What's a Mother (in-law) to Do?

What's a Mother (in-law) to Do?

5 Essential Steps
to Building a
Loving Relationship
with Your Son's New Wife

Jane Angelich

HOWARD BOOKS
A DIVISION OF SIMON & SCHUSTER
New York   London   Toronto   Sydney

Our purpose at Howard Books is to:
Increase faith in the hearts of growing Christians
Inspire holiness in the lives of believers
Instill hope in the hearts of struggling people everywhere
Because He's coming again!

Published by Howard Books, a division of Simon & Schuster, Inc.
1230 Avenue of the Americas, New York, NY 10020
www.howardpublishing.com

Library of Congress Cataloging-in-Publication Data
Angelich, Jane.
    What's a mother (in-law) to do? : five essential steps to building a loving relationship with your son's new wife / Jane Angelich.
        p. cm.
1.   Mothers-in-law—Psychology. 2.   Mothers-in-law—Family relationships. 3.   Family
4.   Interpersonal relations. I. Title.
    HQ759.25.A64 2009
    646.7'8—dc22

                                                                                    2008044982

ISBN: 978-1-4165-8780-4

10   9   8   7   6   5   4   3   2   1

HOWARD colophon is a registered trademark of Simon & Schuster, Inc.

Manufactured in the United States of America.

For information regarding special discounts for bulk purchases, please contact Simon & Schuster Special Sales at 1-866-506-1949 or business@simonandschuster.com.

The Simon & Schuster Speakers Bureau can bring authors to your live event. For more information or to book an event, contact the Simon & Schuster Speakers Bureau at 1-866-248-3049 or visit our website at www.simonspeakers.com.

Edited by Between the Lines
Cover and interior design by Stephanie D. Walker

Scripture taken from the *New American Standard Bible*®, copyright © 1960, 1962, 1963, 1968, 1971, 1972, 1973, 1975, 1977, 1995 by The Lockman Foundation. Used by permission. www.Lockman.org

Amanda, when you got engaged, I told everybody I ran into that my son was marrying a wonderful woman, and I was looking forward to having a great relationship with her.

And that is how this book was born. After congratulations, the reactions to my announcement repeatedly came with a warning. People told me that because most daughters-in-law dislike their mothers-in-law, I should be ready to accept a lackluster relationship at best.

Well, I refused to believe it, since we both love the same person—your husband and my son, Erik.

So I set out to disprove them all by profiling women who have warm, loving relationships with their mothers-in-law, like I had with my late mother-in-law, Dolores. I wanted to find out their secrets for making it work. I figure that if you and I know the formula for a successful relationship, then all three of us—you, Erik, and I—will win.

So, Amanda, this book is a belated wedding gift, dedicated to you. I believe that our relationship will continue to grow closer over the coming years and that your marriage to my son will be as strong and loving as my marriage to my husband, Mark.

Welcome to our family.

Contents

Let us make one point,
that we meet each other with a smile,
when it is difficult to smile.
Smile at each other,
make time for each other
in your family.

—Mother Teresa

Foreword

As deputy editor of WeddingChannel.com, I've become quite accustomed to seeing statements like these on our daily message boards: "I really don't want her there." "If my future husband put his mom before me I would cancel the wedding!" "My mother-in-law is still getting used to me . . . she still has a hard time accepting that her 'baby' is married. She has told me this—I'm not just guessing."

Unfortunately, weddings tend to bring out the best *and* the worst in people. The term "bridezilla" is somewhat new, but the art of dealing with in-laws is actually *really* old news—as in ancient (just check out the Book of Ruth in the Bible and read the account of Ruth and her mother-in-law, Naomi, who had lost her husband and her son). These two women were hit with several adverse situations that could have made them bitter enemies, but they stuck together making their story an incredible example to millions of people over millennia.

What's the moral of the story? Your son or daughter is starting a new chapter in his or her life, and while you may play a supporting role, the spotlight sits squarely on the bride and groom. Most mothers have no problem with that notion— they understand their child's need for space and independence. Unfortunately, it's the few moms out there that struggle with losing control of their children that make every bride hope *her* future MIL isn't actively auditioning for the lead in *Monster-in-Law 2*!

This book offers practical learning tools on how to avoid situations that can cause tension for many years, citing typical mother-in-law/daughter-in-law pitfalls. You'll be challenged to look beneath the surface of your issues and encouraged to offer up respect, honesty, empathy, understanding, and courtesy at every opportunity. Whether you're a mother-in-law already, or just one in training, this book will be your guide to building a better relationship with the newest addition to your family.

—*Summer Krecke, deputy editor, WeddingChannel.com*

Motherhood:

All love begins and ends there.

—Robert Browning

Acknowledgments

Thanks and appreciation to Chrys Howard for her faith in my dream; to my editor, Dawn Brandon, for making my writing life much easier; and to my fabulous agent, Penny Nelson, who has been with me every step of this journey.

And to my family—my dad; my husband, Mark; my terrific sons, Erik and Alex; and my sister, Jill—I couldn't have done it without your love, support, and patience.

Most important, to Amanda: without you, there would be no book to write.

The bonds that link your true family
are not one of blood,
but of respect and joy
in each other's life.
Rarely do members of one family
grow up under the same roof.

—Richard Bach

Introduction

How It All Began

Listen to ten of your married female friends, and you'll soon discover that at least six of them struggle in their relationships with either their mother-in-law or their daughter-in-law. How can it be that in 2008, the mother-in-law/daughter-in-law duo is still one of the most maligned and feared relationships for more than 36 million married women? As 2.4 million women say "I do" each and every year, statistics suggest that more than a million of these new recruits join the army of malcontents waging war against their husband's mother every year. That is such a shame, given that the two women at war were brought together in the first place by their shared love for one man—the son of one and the husband of the other.

What's a Mother (in-Law) to Do? Five Essential Steps to Building a Loving Relationship with Your Son's New Wife began for me on vacation, in a hotel room in Boston, during the 2004 World Series. My husband and I knew that our son, Erik, was going to propose to his girlfriend, Amanda, because he had flown home to California two months earlier to go ring shopping with us. They called us from their home state of Virginia and told us the all details of "popping the question."

> *I wanted to hear directly from the women who have figured out how to tackle the thorny issues of everyday in-law life and come away still liking each other.*

I began calling everyone I knew to tell them the great news that my oldest son was engaged. And that's when it all started: first the congratulations . . . then the warnings. Advice came from all sides—from older women whose sons had wives, from younger women struggling with their mothers-in-law, and from the men who were caught in the middle. From all of them the refrain was the same: enjoy it now, because in time you will become the "monster-in-law."

According to research, nearly 60 percent of all marriages

suffer from tension between mothers-in-law and daughters-in-law. Interestingly, the complaints coming from daughters-in-law are far more varied than those of the mothers-in-law. In fact, the overwhelming response of mothers-in-law was that they did not understand why their daughters-in-law had issues with them.

Knowing that the odds were stacked against me, I was determined not to screw things up but rather to learn how the successful mother-in-law/daughter-in-law relationships had been built—and maintained. Finding answers to my questions would begin with taking advice from the experts. It seems there are zillions of relationship books written by psychologists, psychiatrists, and other relationship gurus who analyze our reasons, methods, and motives in dealing with family members. Rather than just reading about it, I chose to obtain my education first from those who had flourishing and happy relationships with their mothers-in-law. I wanted to hear directly from the women who have figured out how to tackle the thorny issues of everyday in-law life and come away still liking each other. After all, even if a whopping 60 percent of women have troubled relationships with their mothers-in-law, that means 40 percent of them have figured out how to have good ones. And I wanted to learn from them!

Searching for Answers

I began my search for answers by contacting WeddingChannel .com, a leader in the wedding industry and a wholly owned subsidiary of The Knot, Inc. With their assistance I posted a request to interview women who had great relationships with their mothers-in-law.

I received responses from all over the world, ranging from women who were newly engaged to women who had been married for more than forty years. Input came from women of all economic and ethnic backgrounds. It gave me hope that the early "friendly" warnings could be overcome.

> *It gave me hope that the early "friendly" warnings could be overcome.*

I also read Internet postings by women who are anxious to build healthy, loving relationships with their sons' new brides and by those who are already well seasoned in their mother-in-law status but want to improve the dynamic with their daughters-in-law. The audience for this topic is certainly out there, and like me, they are eager to figure out how to navigate these sometimes tricky waters.

After distilling and analyzing the huge volume of data collected from a survey I posted on WeddingChannel.com, it became clear to me that there are five key elements to a successful relationship between a mother and her son's wife.

I then turned to the books and literature on relationships currently available to mothers-in-law. Reading everything I could find on the topic and extracting the professionals' advice further confirmed that these five principles are key to building a successful relationship with your daughter-in-law. With a wealth of personal stories and expert advice in hand, I was ready to write this book and share what I have learned with you.

And, just as important . . . I am ready to assume my new role!

Remembering My Sunday-School Lessons

As I was thinking about mother-in-law and daughter-in-law relationships that had gone right, I remembered a Bible story featuring this very topic. So I went back and took a look at the book of Ruth, one of the shortest books in both Christian and Jewish Scripture. The condensed version of this story goes like this:

During a famine, an Israelite family emigrates from Bethlehem to the nearby country of Moab. After her husband dies, Naomi is left with two sons, who marry two Moabite women, Ruth and Orpah. Then both of Naomi's sons die.

Naomi plans to return to Bethlehem, in Israel, but before she leaves, she tells her widowed daughters-in-law to return to their Moabite homes and remarry. Naomi isn't trying to send them away for selfish reasons but because she knows that she is too old to remarry and doesn't want to be a burden on the younger women. They insist on going with her anyway. Naomi orders them not to follow her, and Orpah finally leaves; but Ruth stays with her, vowing, "Where you go, I will go, and where you lodge, I will lodge. Your people shall be my people, and your God, my God. Where you die, I will die, and there I will be buried" (Ruth 1:16–17).

> *Where you die, I will die, and there I will be buried.*

Naomi and Ruth return to Bethlehem at barley-harvest time. They have no money, so Ruth goes to work in the fields collecting the grain left behind by the harvesters. Ruth doesn't know it yet, but she happens to be working in the fields of Boaz, a relative of Naomi's dead husband. He invites Ruth to drink his water and collect the grain from his fields. She asks him why he's being so kind to a stranger, and he says that he is kind to her because he has heard of her loyalty to her mother-in-law.

Ruth and Boaz eventually marry and have a son. The women of Bethlehem congratulate Naomi, telling her that her daughter-in-law Ruth "is better to you than seven sons" (Ruth 4:15). Naomi becomes a second mother to the boy, who is named Obed, and in the genealogy that concludes this story, we see that Obed is an ancestor to David. The New Testament tells us that Jesus is descended from David, so we see that a high honor—having the promised Messiah come from your family—is bestowed upon Ruth for her kindness to her mother-in-law.

I figure there must have been mother-in-law and daughter-in-law relationship issues dating back thousands of years if an entire book of the Bible is devoted to teaching such an inspirational lesson. Way to go, Ruth and Naomi!

What's Everyone Really Looking For?

Before beginning my own book, I decided to take a look at the reviews written by readers of other books that deal with the issues surrounding mother-in-law and daughter-in-law relationships so I could try to tackle some of their concerns. Keep in mind, however, that almost all of these other books are written from a totally different starting point: addressing relationships involving a sick, dying, or dead mother-in-law, the experts tried to give pointers, primarily to daughters-in-law, on how to give "relationship CPR" and try to make everyone better.

I was also amazed to discover the number of questions on multiple Web sites that revolved around the "bad mother-in-law" and so few that focused on the "bad daughter-in-law." Take a look at this entry, written by a father-in-law defending his wife:

> *I do not know what kind of grandmother/mother-in-law you are, but I can tell you and anyone else who reads this that not every mother-in-law is the wicked witch of the west the world portrays. Do a Google search of mother-in-law/daughter-in-law problems and about all you find are a multitude of Web sites bent on showcasing how stupid, moronic, wicked, evil, disgusting, spawns-of-Satan mothers-in-law are.*

Yes, there are bad mothers-in-law. *Really* bad mothers-in-law. We get it already. There are tons of sites that denigrate mothers-in-law and psycho grandmothers. I am here defending the good ones.

I'm not sure whether my mothers-in-law "group" is oblivious to relationship problems or just not as vocal about them, but I had expected to find the good-versus-evil postings more in balance. I was wrong.

So, because I had much more to work with, I went back to

the daughters-in-law issues. If I hoped to educate mothers-in-law, including myself, on how to succeed in their new role, it was important for me to understand what they're looking for.

I decided to focus on the top five wishes of daughters-in-law, who say they want a book that

- provides a resource for anyone who has mother-in-law trouble and for those who want to know what to do before a problem starts;

- is written in everyday language, not psychological or medical terminology, and that gives real-life examples;

- describes how a good in-law acts;

- gives guidelines that don't take a one-sided approach in favor of the mother-in-law; and

- offers solutions, not a profile of angry women venting about their relationship problems.

The following statement, from a book review, summarized what I was beginning to feel as I embarked on this journey: "There is no way that one person in a relationship involving at least three people can possibly 'fix' it all by themselves."

But I do believe that the mother-in-law, being the older woman (in most cases) with more life experience, is in a position to take the lead. Experience aside, it seems we mothers-in-law would benefit from a little guidance. We could use a tool to help us do a better job in our new role and, as an added bonus, set up the new family member for success in her role as well. A book with tips to achieve these goals—using input from daughters-in-law who weren't "broken" or bitter—was definitely needed.

I've done my best to provide just that. I hope you find this book a useful tool. Maybe you'll decide to share it with your son and daughter-in-law, and together, the three of you can not only prevent (or tackle) the issues that tear at so many families but also create healthy, nurturing relationships that would make Ruth and Naomi proud.

Live in such a way
that you wouldn't be ashamed
to sell your parrot
to the town gossip.

—Will Rogers

Hold Your Tongue
(Let Them Find Their Own Way)

Resisting the Urge to Offer Unsolicited Advice

In his *Stand Still Like the Hummingbird,* author Henry Miller said, "To refrain from giving advice, to refrain from meddling in the affairs of others, to refrain, even though the motives be the highest, from tampering with another's way of life—so simple, yet so difficult for an active spirit! Hands off!"

When you're married to a career coach (me) and, at the age of forty, you express a lifelong desire to be a firefighter (my husband), you change careers. That's the advice I gave my husband, and he says he's thrilled that he took it. So imagine that your business is giving advice, and you learn that the number-one factor in mother-in-law/daughter-in-law relationships crumbling is giving advice! The problem seems to lie in giving unsolicited advice, and I know it will be challenging for me to refrain from saying what I think. After all, I have years of experience as a wife, as a parent, and as a person of the world. Isn't it my right (even my responsibility!) to share the wisdom gleaned over so many years? Survey says . . . no!

> Do I have to walk on eggshells, or bite my tongue every time we speak?

But what if my daughter-in-law does ask for advice? How can I give it and still maintain a loving relationship over the years? Do I have to walk on eggshells or bite my tongue every time we speak? And what if I misinterpret a statement as a question and end up sharing my thoughts on her career or home decorating, their children or holiday traditions? In that situation, have I crossed the line? How do I know when she might appreciate my stepping in and when she would resent it? If I do dare throw in my two cents, will I end up just another statistic, lumped in with those mothers-in-law who inspire an endless number of bad jokes and horror stories? Why is it so hard for us to shut our mouths, anyway?

As those questions buzz around in my mind, I remember what many of the daughters-in-law from the survey said: in essence, "Trust us. Let us make our own mistakes. We know you have wisdom, but we want to build our own wisdom through trial and error."

And so I move forward, holding fast to essential rule number one: try not to offer (too much) unsolicited advice.

Avoid Prewedding Bitters

Beginning with the wedding planning process, it's tempting to offer advice. After all, you are the mother of the groom. I lived three thousand miles away from my son and future daughter-in-law, and I still worried about how to balance being involved in the planning without being intrusive. Add to that my absolute passion for weddings (I probably would be a wedding planner if I wasn't a career coach), and I had a recipe for disaster.

I was already one foot (in mouth) into dangerous territory when Amanda and Erik were selecting their wedding date. I knew my son wanted a 2006 wedding, but I also knew that Amanda was shooting for 2005. I listened to Erik's reasoning, which was logical: he was finishing up an MBA program in 2005 and wanted to get it behind him before the wedding. I listened to Amanda's reasoning, which also was logical: she would be doing most of the planning, and they could delay their honeymoon until after graduation. I was glad I lived three time zones away, and I secretly hoped nobody asked me what I thought.

Since this first test of tongue control came before my book research began, I didn't have the benefit of my own advice experts to guide me through this potential mine field. Luckily, I somehow sensed that giving advice, solicited or not, on the first big decision of their engagement was a no-no.

So, when I was asked what I thought, I stepped squarely up to the plate . . . and circumvented the issue by letting them know that I would be happy with either decision.

When I think back on my seemingly wishy-washy response, the truth is that I would have been happy with either decision; but I'm even happier that they reached one on their own (they got married in 2005).

My decision to act as a sounding board rather than an advisory board was the right way to go. So far, so good. Sometimes, however, tensions can run high, as can the potential for misinterpreted comments and hurt feelings. The excitement and stress of planning a wedding may create situations for couples and their extended families that don't resemble "real life." Some postings on the Internet illustrated this truth:

My soon-to-be mother-in-law is making me crazy! She calls every few weeks to tell us she's angry about something involving the wedding and won't come. Then the next week she calls back to say she's sorry. I'm sick of it.

Here's another:

My fiancé's family is driving me crazy. Ever since we announced our engagement, they've been bombarding me on all sides with demands—from inviting third cousins to including their kids in the ceremony! They're creating so much craziness that I'm ready to give up on the whole wedding and elope.

One woman wrote:

This may sound kind of funny, but I am having trouble with my future mother-in-law trying to save us too much money on the wedding. I knew even before I met my fiancé what kind of wedding I wanted, and I am more than willing to pay the extra money for it! It's getting to the point where I can't even tell her anything about the wedding, because she will replace all my ideas with cheaper ones! I really like my fiancé's mother, and I don't want to hurt her feelings, but this is getting annoying!

Uh-oh . . . words like *crazy, annoying,* and *elope* can't be a good way to get started. A good mother-in-law/daughter-in-law relationship is built over time, and patience on both sides is important at this early stage.

Lisa D. told me about an early misstep she made with her

soon-to-be mother-in-law. Because they both had established some trust between them and were generous in their interpretations of the other, what could have become a sore spot in their relationship did not. Here's Lisa's story:

"I have no intention of getting married more than once." As soon as I hit the Send button on my computer, I knew that I had blown it. Caught up in the excitement of wedding planning, I sent my DIVORCED AND REMARRIED future mother-in-law, Barbara, an e-mail about getting the details right and, without giving it a second thought, added the line about one marriage and one marriage only.

> *Barbara's good judgment in supporting the couple during the ups and downs of planning a wedding, . . . was the right way to embark on the new relationship with her daughter-in-law.*

I thought, Oh, no, I'll bet she sees that as some kind of criticism about her. How was this going to play out? Was she going to hold a grudge and challenge every decision we made, starting with the wedding plans?

Right away I apologized for the off-hand remark and told Barbara that I thought she and I were close enough that she would know where my comment was coming from.

I've saved her e-mail back to me. She told me not to think twice about the comment because she knew what was in my heart.

Rather than holding onto the remark and stewing about it, Barbara chose to respond immediately and to remind Lisa that she understood the bigger picture. The only husband Lisa ever wanted was Barbara's son, and that should please any mother of the groom.

Lisa recognized the potential danger and deeply appreciated Barbara's response. She wrote:

With another new mother-in-law, this could have started a feud; but because of the trust that the two of us have, we moved past it. She proved to me then and there that a successful mother-in-law sees her children and their spouses as well-meaning, even if they say something wrong.

Lisa went on to say:

My mother-in-law was a soothing, constant source of support throughout our engagement and wedding planning process— she was confident in OUR decisions and prepared to support them . . . even if she may have had ideas of her own that were different and despite my careless remark!

Barbara's good judgment in supporting the couple during the ups and downs of planning a wedding, regardless of whether she agreed with all of the decisions, was the right way to embark on the new relationship with her daughter-in-law.

Let Her Find Her Own Way— Even If It's Different from Yours

I got married (the first time) on my twentieth birthday. Later I graduated from college and I got a job. I worked full-time, outside of the home, while raising my children and took a lot of heat from a lot of people for doing so. I was part of that first wave of women in the 1970s who "did it all." But I kept a mental script of responses ready for whenever someone challenged me about my work/life balance. I hated having to justify my life choices by using the script. And so does every woman who wants to find her own way. Those starting out in marriage and building a family want to feel that their choices are accepted without judgment. And the mother-in-law who can embrace her daughter-in-law's path, though it may be different from her own, will be cherished.

Anna, a law-school administrator from California, won't need a script for her mother-in-law. She wrote this about Judy, whom she has known for over six years:

I am so impressed by her . . . my mother-in-law successfully raised three great kids, leaving her first career as a pharmacist to begin her second career as a homemaker. . . .

Unlike so many Chinese moms I have known, she did not get upset when I decided to keep my maiden name or when I decided to keep working when we had kids.

Although she lives only a few minutes away, she is never pushing unwanted advice or being intrusive or nosy—but still she will always offer help if we ask her! Judy has always made me feel like she is genuinely happy that I'm the one who married her only son.

Quite a testimonial to a traditional mother-in-law whose only son is practically her neighbor! By not criticizing Anna's choices, Judy has opened a wide door of trust and sent the message that she respects her daughter-in-law.

In another situation, Colette, a writer from Pennsylvania, married Jeff after knowing him for about a month. Here again, different goals between the daughter-in-law and mother-in-law, yet no problems. After more than ten years of marriage, Collette has this to say about her mother-in-law, Sally:

"Do what is best for the two of you." I have to admit that if I found out that my son was about to marry a woman he'd known for only five weeks, I might not have led with that advice. But since Sally knew that Jeff wanted to marry me, she accepted me

immediately and has treated me like a friend. She has shown me from day one that even though I have very different goals than the ones she had at my age, she supports us. I really want to thank her for still being genuinely glad to hear my voice when I call.

In some families a mother-in-law can provide lots of "advice" while not saying a word. And that can be a good thing! Kerri, who has a PhD in electrical engineering, says she learns volumes just watching her mother-in-law, Lois, handle situations with other family members, including Kerri's husband. By observing Lois's communication and timing, Kerry has figured out when to say something to her husband and when it might be wiser to hold off and bring it up in another context. She wrote this about her relationship with Lois:

I am so honored to have another woman in my life whose experience I can draw upon. It seems like both of us try not to sweat the small stuff and focus more energy on developing the big picture, slowly and surely, making sure that everyone is comfortable with the end goals. We are both high-energy and independent women, and I think we mesh well and agree on the fundamentals of what it means to be a family. We don't internalize so much as vocalize . . . as tactfully and respectfully as we know how and as loudly as we need to in order to make sure we're being heard.

Kerri taught me that walking on eggshells is not the path to achieving a great mother-in-law/daughter-in-law relationship. By observing her mother-in-law, she was able to glean important bits of information from her actions. Kerri says, "There isn't any sense of what I 'should' or 'shouldn't' do with respect to her son and our life choices, and the trust that implies is much appreciated."

Kerri and Lois's story also showed me that sometimes my interactions with my son may be just enough information for my daughter-in-law to pick up on my feelings about a subject. If you do speak up, make sure that the important goal of maintaining a caring relationship is kept at the forefront in order to keep the lines of communication open between the two of you.

Am I on the Right Path?

As a true romantic, I believe in love at first sight. When I met my current husband, I knew that I was going to marry him. And seventeen years later, I am still as excited to wake up and see him next to me as I was when I met him.

I am also realistic. I know that most people do not succeed in marriage using this approach. The same goes for my budding relationship with my new daughter-in-law. The "romantic" side of me wants to say, "This is my new best friend, Amanda." But I know that, in reality, our friendship needs to grow over time.

All of us have an emotional side, and all human beings are capable of changing. Great mother-in-law/daughter-in-law relationships are built on caring, not on power and control. Before she loves you, she has to like you. So how can you know if you're succeeding at building a rich and rewarding relationship with your daughter-in-law?

The answer is much clearer to me now than it was before I began writing this book. There's nothing wrong with constructive advice if it is asked for and if it is designed to enhance the relationship. It's all in the approach. When I'm tempted to offer advice, I think about the way I would give advice to my friends. Along the continuum of friendship, how would I offer advice to a new friend? What would I say to my best friend? To my sister? Right now, your new daughter-in-law (or the daughter-in-law with whom you would like to have a better relationship) is a new friend, and suggestions and advice need to be handled accordingly. So if she decides her heart is set on a wedding dress or job you don't care for, better to tread gently,

> *There's nothing wrong with constructive advice if it is asked for and if it is designed to enhance the relationship.*

just as you would with a new friend. You may think of her as family. But she may not feel that way yet.

The experts have taught me that we have to let our daughters-in-law make their own way in the world, mistakes and all, just like we did when we were starting out. As a mother-in-law, you have to keep track of where you are on the continuum of friendship to gauge the amount and type of advice you can offer without ruffling feathers. If you remain sensitive to that and can control the urge to speak your mind and correct every step of the way, then you may be fortunate enough to have a relationship like Lisa D. and her in-laws, especially her mother-in-law, Barbara:

> As I was preparing for Thanksgiving this year, I was reminded of how fortunate I am to have three special "mothers." I have my mother, who cried as she walked into our new home, saw the table set, and was overcome with pride. I have my husband's stepmother, who gave us our dining-room table as a wedding gift. And I have Barbara, my husband's biological mother, whose exquisite set of hand-painted china adorned the table. There was no better representation of our special situation than that holiday table.
>
> In the eighteen months that we have been married, I regard myself as the luckiest newlywed around. My in-laws are the ideal complement to my own mother, who is amazing in her

own right. *They have allowed us to lead our own lives, with no demands, no expectations, and nothing but acceptance, support, and love.*

Because I was raised in an interfaith family where both Hanukkah and Christmas are celebrated, it has been important to me to share as much of my family and my culture as possible with them. When we visited Barbara in Wisconsin for the holidays, Hanukkah and Christmas fell during the same week. Knowing the importance of both holidays to me, she created a Hanukkah meal that included brisket and her famous German potato pancakes, which she renamed "latkes." And my stepfather-in-law presented a menorah that he had made out of wood and thick candles that he uses when staying at his hunting lodge. It was a very meaningful Hanukkah, Sheboygan style!

All brides should be so lucky, and all families should have such a wonderful start.

Can It Last a Lifetime?

I often wonder if it's possible to sustain a great relationship for decades, which would involve a lot of "think before you speak" restraint in the advice department. Sandy, a spa manager who knew her late mother-in-law, Jennie, for more than forty years, sums it up this way:

We knew each other for over forty years, saw each other almost every day, and although she is gone, I want everyone to know that she loved me like one of her own children. She never judged, never gave unsolicited advice, and always listened with an open mind and heart and offered support. My mother-in-law showed me by those actions that she respected me. And she reminded me that all women are not alike, that I should always be myself, and that my relationship with my husband, her son, involved just the two of us.

By loving me the way she did, she made me love my husband even more.

These women are living proof that great relationships—even those between mother-in-law and daughter-in-law—really can last a lifetime.

What I Learned:
The Irk Factor Can Be Minimized

When I think back to the early years of my first marriage, I still remember some of my mother-in-law's comments and advice that irked me. But thirty plus years later, I can honestly say that none of it was so horrific that it ruined our relationship—even though I've been divorced from her son for a long time.

My goal as a new mother-in-law is to minimize the "irk factor" for my daughter-in-law. Every woman I interviewed while writing this book acknowledged that her mother-in-law knew just what to say and when to say it. Here's what they taught me: it doesn't matter if you live next door or thousands of miles away; she keeps her name or takes his; you each chose different career paths; your culture, faith, or traditions don't match; or your relationship is a few weeks or a few decades long. If you respect your daughter-in-law, listen to her, trust her, and let her make her own mistakes, she will be truly glad to hear your voice.

The Experts Weigh In

In order to save you the time of reading all those zillions of expert books, I spoke with a variety of relationship professionals and did a lot of reading. Based on all of that expertise, here are some of the questions you need to ask yourself in order to determine whether you might be heading down the path to becoming Queen of Unsolicited Advice.

Do you . . .

- believe most people need your care?

- think you know what is best in most situations?

- tell people what they should think and how they should feel?

- offer advice and directions without being asked?

- become resentful when people don't want your help?

- feel uninterested in other people's ideas?

If any of this sounds like you, the next step is to understand why you feel compelled to speak your mind—and to learn some proven ways to get back on track.

Why You Might Be Behaving This Way

Let's take a look at some of the insights offered by experts:

- You may have a wealth of experience that you want to share with others. If you have been "around the block" so to speak, it makes sense that you would want to help others avoid similar pitfalls.

- It isn't easy inviting a new person into your life, especially one who is going to be so close with your beloved son. Offering advice can be a way of feeling needed, included, and indispensable.

- It's hard to give up control. You may have a sense that everything familiar is going to change; that your son, who has always needed you, has found someone else to give him support and advice. Giving advice may serve as a way to cope with the anxiety that accompanies such a huge life transition. Change can create fear and a sense of loss. There are many underlying reasons for needing to control a situation by offering unsolicited advice. Some of them are jealousy, a subconscious feeling of sadness over "losing" your son, the feeling that you need to compete with your daughter-in-law for attention, and even regrets about your own relationship with your mother-in-law.

Why Change?

There are some really good reasons to spend some time working on changing your ways. Here are just a few:

- Unsolicited advice can sabotage relationships.

- People don't always welcome the advice they receive. The advice might be insightful and even good, but it could be resented nonetheless. It's not always a matter of your intentions but how your actions are perceived.

- Seemingly innocent questions and statements expressing genuine interest or concern may be thinly disguised, unsolicited advice that may bring unintended consequences. For example, you say: "Why don't you call Mary for some tips on dressing for your new job—she always looks so nice." On the surface, you think you're helping by giving your daughter-in-law a source for a wardrobe consult. But underneath that advice is the not-so-subtle hint that your daughter-in-law doesn't have good taste in clothing and that you don't approve of her appearance.

- Ask yourself: What is the goal? Do you want a loving relationship with your daughter-in-law? If so, imagine how it must feel trying to merge into a group (your family) with already long-established relationships. Imagine what some of your daughter-in-law's worries might be: Will I be liked? What if I'm not? Will I fit in? Will I have to sacrifice my ideals to be accepted? Will my husband support me? The prospect can be intimidating and the pressure overwhelming. How can you help your daughter-in-law feel comfortable enough to be herself, let down her defenses, and find a place in your family and in your hearts?

Some Conditions That Make Us Feel Welcome

- We don't feel judged.

- We feel that people are interested in who we are, how we feel, and what we believe in.

- We feel we have space to evolve and become connected with others.

- We feel validated and respected.

- We feel that there's room to make mistakes.

- We feel that it's all right to be different.

- We are treated fairly.

As the mother-in law you play a vital role in creating a safe, welcoming, and open environment—or not. One sure barrier to creating a wonderful relationship with your daughter-in-law is offering unsolicited advice.

Seven Simple Suggestions for Success

1. Analyze your motives before giving advice, and make sure you have the other person's best interests at heart.

2. Ask yourself if your advice might hurt your daughter-in-law's feelings. Would it hurt yours if roles were reversed?

3. Listen respectfully, especially in emotionally charged situations.

4. Try to figure out how your daughter-in-law will perceive the significance of what is being said in light of her circumstances.

5. Look beyond your position. Take the opportunity to learn more about who your daughter-in-law is and how she sees things.

6. Remember that even if you do know what's best, part of a couple's development is learning through mistakes.

7. If you want to be helpful, consider asking questions like these:

   • What do you think is the right thing to do?

- What do you see as the problem?

- How do you think this will impact your life?

- Have you thought about what you might do?

- What is the worst thing you can imagine happening?

- How does that make you feel?

- Why does that bother you?

These questions will help validate others, making them feel that you have faith in how they think and problem-solve. And if they haven't made a decision, often these questions will help clarify in their own minds what they need to do—without your having to tell them.

One Final Tip

Changing familiar behavior patterns is difficult. For some, reading this book may be enough of a catalyst to start breaking unhelpful habits. For others, more outside support may be helpful. You might seek support from friends, a spouse, or a therapist. It is a sign of strength, not weakness, to seek support during these major life transitions.

Say little, and love much;
give all; judge no man,
aspire to all that is
pure and good.

—White Eagle

Embrace Her!
(But Give Her Room to Breathe)

Letting Her Become Part of the Family at Her Own Pace

I met my first mother-in-law when I was eighteen and a college freshman; she was thirty-eight and a high-school teacher. About two months after meeting her, I became engaged to her son. Talk about speed dating, I probably could have won an award in that department. The interesting thing about that time in my life is that my future mother-in-law was a wholehearted advocate of the marriage, while my own parents thought (but didn't tell me until I was divorced twenty years later) that I was nuts for wanting to marry so young. I was accepted into my husband's family—including my two future brothers-in-law, ages thirteen and eight—unconditionally.

As the years went by, nothing changed significantly in my mother-in-law's behavior, but *my* behavior did change. Looking back on it now, I thinks I was so in love with the idea of getting married that I would have gotten along with Lizzie Borden if that got me to the wedding. But once I had that ring on my finger, I started to find little things that annoyed me about my mother-in-law and used them as a basis for complaints.

> *My in-laws wanted to maximize their time with us by having intellectual discussions about world events, but I felt like a prisoner and wanted a time-out.*

Let me give you an example of one that I remember, keeping in mind that it has been a long time since I was her daughter-in-law. Whenever my first husband and I went to visit his parents, we spent almost the entire time in the house with them. We didn't get in the car and go for a drive or out to lunch. We stayed in the living room . . . and watching TV was not an option.

My in-laws wanted to maximize their time with us by having intellectual discussions about world events, but I felt like a prisoner and wanted a time-out. When I was growing up, the conversations in my home centered around television programs and whom we saw at the mall that day. My mother was a stay-at-home mom and my mother-in-law was a working mom . . . our homes were just different.

What should have happened from the start of that marriage is a "somewhere in the middle" approach to visiting my mother-in-law. I can't fault her for wanting to spend time with us and for being a smart woman who was knowledgeable about world events. Neither was there anything wrong with my desire to get some air periodically and to turn on the TV. We just needed to find the middle ground. Despite her best intentions, I felt suffocated.

Looking back, my husband could have helped us. He knew her. He knew me. If he saw the situation and had put his finger on the problem, lots of tension could have been relieved much earlier on. After all, lots of love should never be a problem. But we can encounter problems if no one ever addresses how that love is expressed.

I do believe it's possible to successfully welcome your daughter-in-law into your family. Both of my mothers-in-law proved that to me. But I wonder if my acceptance of my new daughter-in-law will be reciprocated. Is it much harder for a daughter-in-law to enter the unknown kingdom of her in-laws than it is to hold the keys to this kingdom? What will she expect? Will I be aware of her expectations early enough in the relationship to prevent what happened to me in my first encounter with the queen of that other kingdom many years ago? Might a good or bad beginning depend on something as simple as what I expect her to call me?

Call Me Mom!

When I met my first mother-in-law, I didn't know what to call her. I was still a kid myself and had been raised to address my parents' friends respectfully as Mrs. or Mr. [last name] . . . so I started there. But my mother-in-law insisted that *Mrs.* was too formal. Unfortunately, she gave me only one other option: calling her Mom.

I couldn't do it. I had one mother in my life, and I reserved *Mom* for her. I wasn't comfortable using it to address my mother-in-law. So, for eighteen years, I called her nothing. When I wanted her attention, I would just start talking or wait until she was looking at me. Sounds ridiculous now, but it made sense then. It was one of those things that went on for so long that I couldn't figure a way out of it.

When I met my current husband's mother, I was much older and she introduced herself by her first name. And that's what I called her. Inside I breathed a sigh of relief that she didn't start down the Mom path again, though I think that by that point in my life I would have been able to tell her that I reserved that name for my mother but that any other alternative would be fine.

Sometimes, even when you start with *Mom*, problems can arise when that doesn't seem to be working anymore, as evidenced by this Web posting: "Two years of calling her 'Mom,' and I get a birthday card, and she signed it with her first name, not 'Mom.' Now I feel dumb. Two years later? How?"

It's important to remember that as your son's new spouse, your daughter-in-law has suddenly gained a whole new family. To expect instant bonding is probably unrealistic. And delving directly to "Mom-calling" may be too big a leap—initially or ever.

> *It's important to remember that your daughter-in-law has suddenly gained a whole new family. To expect instant bonding is probably unrealistic.*

KimChi, a filmmaker and journalist in her forties, says she handled the delicate situation and transitioned into her new family this way:

After we got married, she used to call and say on the message machine, "Hi, Berny and KimChi, this is Mom." I got used to the phrase and started calling her Mom, but it felt a little weird at first. Weeks later she asked me, "Do you feel weird calling me

Mom?" *I thought it was very observant that she picked that up, and I answered her honestly.*

It's admirable that KimChi's mother-in-law was astute enough to read the signs of discomfort and that KimChi was comfortable enough to respond truthfully. Now when she calls her mother-in-law Mom, KimChi feels good about it. She was given the opportunity to express her opinion and feels like she had a voice in this important matter.

We all have memories, good or bad, of how it felt to transition into a new family as the daughter-in-law. Now, as mothers-in-law, we have an opportunity. We can use our own experience, along with the insights from others in this chapter, to learn how we can make that transition better and easier for our new family members.

> Sometimes geography plays a big role in the level of difficulty for a daughter-in-law to join in and feel like part of a family.

The first time I met my daughter-in-law, she came to California over the holidays and stayed with us for a few days. I introduced myself by my first name, which stuck, and she called me by name for more than five years. I have no intention of suggesting that she call me anything else, but I'll certainly be all ears if she comes up with an alternative. Right now, this works for us.

Is This Really a Welcome Mat?

I think welcoming a new daughter-in-law into the family is something like bringing home a new baby. You don't really know what to expect, don't want to make rookie mistakes, and do want to form a loving bond that will last a lifetime. There's so much potential to explore, you can't wait to get going. After all, you managed to raise the son she fell in love with, so why shouldn't it be just as easy to bring her on board?

Sometimes this can make us a bit overzealous; but sometimes the fear of making mistakes leads us to distance ourselves too much. While it's important to give our new daughter-in-law breathing room and not suffocate her as we absorb her into the family, we do need to be sure we don't leave her out in the cold. It's our job to make sure she knows that she's wanted. I felt a pang of sadness when I read this posting on the Internet and tried to imagine starting off with a new family as described:

I am having difficulty in becoming a part of my husband's family life after getting married. Two years ago my husband and I decided to move to his hometown to make a living. I feel as if they have not made as much of an effort to integrate me into the family as they have their other daughter-in-law, "Mary."

It started during the planning of our wedding, when I felt that my mother-in-law did not seem too excited about the wedding and didn't help to plan it. We lived in different states, which might have been a part of it, and also my husband is a very independent person. But I feel that I did many things to try to show I loved and respected his mother and his family.

The pain really took hold last month, when I was looking at a photo album with a copy of my mother-in-law's Christmas letter, which stated how happy she was that "Mary" was her new daughter-in-law and how she wished them the best marriage together. But the year of our own wedding, her Christmas letter barely even mentioned the wedding.

Both of my mothers-in-law had only sons, no daughters. So did I, so none of us got to do girlish things with our children. I loved when my friends had daughters because it meant I could buy gifts with "buttons and bows" instead of the monotonous supply of jeans and T-shirts for my boys.

When my son got engaged, in addition to writing this book as a gift to my future daughter-in-law, I decided to throw a tea party for her family and friends. I can't tell you how much fun I had putting together that party, and I think it was well received. There's nothing like dressing up in your Sunday best, heading off to a tearoom with a group of women, and handing out miniature teddy bears with party hats as favors to bring out the girl in you.

For me the prospect of having another girl in the family was exciting. Judging by these comments, I am not alone.

In New York City, Missy says of her mother-in-law:

We are similar in many ways. Not only does she look like she could be my mom, but we have similar personalities. We enjoy shopping and going to spas together. We have been this way from the beginning. I felt an instant connection with her. She never had a daughter, so with me she has gotten to be girly. She and my father-in-law have included me in family discussions about the future, which helps me to feel very much like an important part of the family.

Ah, shopping excursions and spa days! Sometimes, though, geography prohibits such activities and plays a big role in the level of difficulty for a daughter-in-law to join in and feel like part of a family. Take Michelle, a language consultant in her midforties who currently resides in Italy but didn't start out there. She says:

My poor mother-in-law thought that she was losing her son when we announced we were getting married, because we also announced that we would live in California right after the wedding. This we did, until 1.5 years after, when we made the decision to return to Italy. The only time I ever saw my mother-in-law cry was when I left her home after the wedding. In spite of that, she never made me feel guilty or held a grudge.

> *She never meddled in our affairs, but always made herself available to talk.*

When my husband went back to Italy to rent a house and get things ready for us to live there, his mother took many steps to make it as comfortable as possible, down to fresh flowers in the new house when I arrived. More recently she has included me in the family through gifts of family heirlooms, all symbols of investment in me and in my daughters.

As hard as it was for Michelle's mother-in-law to wave goodbye, she did not take it out on her daughter-in-law. So everyone won when the family returned to Italy and set up residence in the same town as the in-laws.

Tiffany, a loyalty-marketing executive, shared a similarly positive experience:

My mom-in-law has been a cheerleader for me in every way since I met her son sixteen years ago. He and I grew up together and were high-school sweethearts. She has championed my career and academic goal of earning an MBA. She supported our out-of-state move to achieve these goals even though she loved that her son and I lived less than fifteen minutes away for the first seven years of our marriage.

Successfully embracing your daughter-in-law is clearly possible. But there's no magic combination of traits, no secret formula to help her fit in with a family that didn't raise her. Each situation is unique, as we can see from the stories told by these ten women:

Stephanie, a home day-care provider, says:

When I was engaged, my fiancé and I were a little stressed about how much everything was costing and not sure how we would come up with some of the money to pay for things. At Christmas that year I was given a box, and as I was opening it, I began to realize that this wasn't just an ordinary gift. After opening three more boxes and one bag, all packed in the original box, I found the receipt for my wedding dress! I was totally blown away by this because my mother-in-law never even talked about doing this at all. I felt like I was getting the best future in-laws in the entire world.

Kathy, an event planner, shares this insight:

I have known my mother-in-law almost as long as I have known my husband, which is fourteen years. Although we have been married for three years, she has really witnessed me growing up and the relationship evolving. Now that I think about it, I think she is so respectful and great because she struggled in her relationship with her own mother-in-law.

Elizabeth, a legal recruiting manager, says:

My mother-in-law and I have always gotten along very well, from the first day we met at my husband's (then boyfriend's) college graduation fifteen years ago. She welcomed me with open arms, and during the year-long period that her son and I were broken up, she continued to communicate with me and offer comfort. She never meddled in our affairs but always made herself available to talk.

Janet, a medical doctor, gives this account:

At first I thought this woman was bizarre. She continually welcomed me into her life, and I didn't really want a close relationship. I came from two very selfish parents who had children and then didn't think they had to do much to raise them. But my mother-in-law, Robin, wore me down with kindness. Gradually it became a strong bond, and she looked to me for medical, Internet, and technology advice and, in return, took me to plays and shows and a lot of other fun activities.

When my beloved fifteen-year-old cat became quite ill and I needed to let him go, Robin supported me through all of this and helped me let him go.

Maggie, a teacher, says:

I have been part of the family since day one. My mother-in-law makes everyone who walks into her house feel welcome. Half of my husband's friends practically grew up in his house because my mother-in-law never just makes dinner for five but more like ten, just in case anyone unexpected stops over. One thing my mother-in-law did for me to really make me feel part of the family was to cook special things for me when I was pregnant. I was not able to cook, and many things would turn my stomach, so she cooked special, just so I was able to eat.

Lydie, a business owner, says:

We have always had a great relationship. My mother died when I was ten, and my mother-in-law entered my life when I was seventeen. I have been part of the family since day one.

Anna, a law-school administrator, reports:

She has welcomed me with open arms and never once tried to control the relationship. I felt nervous about meeting her after having met past boyfriends' mothers who were very protective about their sons. I truly believe she is the best mother-in-law and count myself lucky to have such a wonderful "second mom."

Jennifer B., founder and designer of a postmaternity garment business, reveals:

I was so scared to meet my mother-in-law. She was bigger than life to me. I heard how religious she is and how we'd have to sleep in separate bedrooms when we visited as boyfriend/girlfriend, even though her son was forty and I was thirty-nine. Still, that made me love her all the more. I love her rules of respect. I love that she has a picture of the Pope hung up in the hallway of her house. And I love that she's done such an amazing job helping influence my husband, who, seriously, is an angel here on earth.

Laurel, a florist, says:

I was immediately welcomed into her family circle and was never made to feel like an outsider. She had a wonderful relationship with her own parents that I was also privileged to enjoy.

And Lara, a lawyer, tells us:

We have always gotten along very well, which I think is surprising because my husband and his mother are very close. We have a fabulous relationship but I do not feel like I am her daughter, nor does she think of me as a daughter. Her number one is her son, so my relationship with her depends on my relationship with her son. We adore each other, but we know our roles.

Ten very successful outcomes from ten very different scenarios, all demonstrating that the old saying, "You're not losing a son; you're gaining a daughter," can really come true.

As my daughter-in-law and I go through life joined together by the same guy, I want her to feel like my door is always open to her. But she gets to choose when she wants to cross that threshold. I know how difficult the early years of marriage can be and how important it is for my son and daughter-in-law to succeed, first and foremost, as a couple.

Let's Do Everything Together! (Dealing with Holidays, Celebrations, and Vacations)

My only sister and I are very close and spent almost every Christmas, Thanksgiving, and any other recognized holiday and celebration with our parents during our entire first marriages. And there were a lot of vacations thrown in there too. According to us, it had to be that way, and our first husbands went along with it. Kudos to them, and shame on us. Now that

I'm married for the second time, I'm embarrassed to admit that the word *compromise* didn't seem to be part of my vocabulary back then.

Every family has its own way of handling holidays, celebrations, and vacations: learning your daughter-in-law's family traditions as well as letting her know about yours are important steps that will help you to better manage the expectations of everyone involved.

My second husband's late mother loved Thanksgiving. It was "her holiday," and she began planning for it in October. We spent all Thanksgivings with her. Christmas was my mother's favorite holiday, but she lived in Florida and was in declining health, and my mother-in-law was a widow in declining health. When you mix together those ingredients, you need creativity coupled with compromise to find a workable solution. One year, when my mother-in-law could still travel, we brought her to Florida. Other years, we celebrated Christmas in Florida but had an earlier celebration with my mother-in-law back in California.

> The key to a successful relationship with your daughter-in-law is recognizing her role in your son's life . . .

When I was doing my online research, reading stories by disgruntled daughters-in-law who were having problems regarding family celebrations, I had to laugh at the first line of the following post: *"My father is a retired NYC police officer and has always said the holidays tend to bring out the crazies in people."* Maybe this is the real reason things seem to get out of control in some families, as this daughter-in-law goes on to explain:

This is certainly true with my mother-in-law. I live in my husband's country (Canada). My family and friends are all in New York or Florida, and I'm lucky if I see my parents three times a year due to finances. My family is extremely close, and we all get along great. My husband's family . . . not so much.

We see hubby's family for Easter, Mother's Day, mother in law's birthday, and Thanksgiving without fail every year. I think it's only fair we see my family for Christmas, since my parents don't get to see me for their birthdays or any other holiday and never complain about it. We explained this to his mother several times from October on. And from October until we went to Florida, his mother called my husband to complain about Christmas and me and how I was being such a baby wanting to see my family.

My husband called his mother to say Merry Christmas to her on Christmas Eve, and she was so rude and nasty to him on the phone that he was upset the entire evening. She's only happy when everyone else is miserable. When we did get back from Florida and went to visit, we bought her a very generous gift that she snubbed and said she didn't need. She insulted me to the point where I cried the whole way home, so now, no more. I'm done with the entire wretched affair.

My mother, knowing how much I dread being around that woman, was kind enough to foot the bill for my plane fare, and I will be spending a stress-free Easter with them. Unfortunately, hubby won't be able to go. I feel so bad for him stuck with such a toxic family.

It appears that an equitable solution isn't part of the life-vocabulary of this family. But some women have figured out solutions to potentially sticky situations in ways that work for everyone involved. Here are some of them:

All holidays are at our house,
with both sides of the family.
—*Anna W.*

We do Christmas early with my family, and then
the actual holiday is spent with my in-laws. We do
Thanksgiving at our house and invite everyone here.
—*Heather*

Early on in the marriage, we established a flexible
guideline that either Christmas or Thanksgiving

would be spent with my mother-in-law.
Now, because my father moved close to us,
all holidays are spent at home, and we include both
my dad and my mother-in-law.
—*Elizabeth*

We usually spend Thanksgiving with my family and
Easter with his. For Christmas we split our time
between each family, depending on the activity/day.
—*Kiley*

My family lives here in New York City, and
my in-laws are in Indiana. My mother-in-law is an
amazingly friendly and sociable person. She is usually
the icebreaker and the person who can sit and talk to
everyone and automatically puts people at ease.
This translates into an open and fun relationship
between my in-laws and my parents as well
as with my entire huge, extended family.
Because they get along extremely well with my family,
holidays are usually all of us together.
—*Missy*

We do every other year split with the holidays.
—*Kerri*

My daughter-in-law's mother lives much closer to her than
I do, and when it comes to holidays, she and my son spend

time with her mom. I am perfectly okay with that because, as I've gotten older, I have come to the realization that it isn't the actual day of the holiday that's important to me. The celebration for me is in spending time with my family, whenever it works for all of us. And the added benefit of not flying during the busiest times of the year is icing on the cake.

Vacations are treated differently in my second marriage than in my first. Being older and working outside of the corporate environment, my husband and I no longer have to worry about how to allocate our two, three, or four weeks of vacation. That gives us much more freedom when deciding where we'll go and whom we'll spend time with during our vacations.

We love to travel and need no convincing to visit new places or relatives. But we do make sure that we take vacations every year that include nobody but us. We believe it's important to our relationship to spend time alone as a couple.

I think it's important to remember that most couples have a limited number of vacation days each year and that they do need to have their own time to get "reacquainted."

Our family-visit vacations probably are not going to be regularly scheduled events. My husband and I sometimes visit my son and daughter-in-law in Washington, D.C.; my daughter-in-law has visited us in California (both with and without my son, as she likes to travel and he doesn't); and all of us met once in Hawaii to celebrate our wedding anniversary. When these things work out, it's great, and I look forward to spending time with my daughter-in-law the next time our schedules match—without demanding that they do.

What I Learned: The Family Circle Always Has Room for New Members

The key to a successful relationship with your daughter-in-law is recognizing her role in your son's life and choosing to be inclusive (without suffocating her) when it comes to bringing her into the fold.

The Experts Weigh In

I learned from my reading that everyone fears being displaced. Therefore, it's important to recognize when you might be sending signals to your daughter-in-law that she is not really considered part of the family.

Do you . . .

- communicate with your daughter-in-law only (or mostly) through your son?

- compete with your daughter-in-law or her family members for your son's attention or affection?

- assume that important holidays should be celebrated in your home, the way it always was when your son was a child?

- expect that you will be included in your son and daughter-in-law's family vacations?

If any of these hit a little too close to home, then it's time to consider what's going on under the surface.

Why You Might Be Behaving This Way

When you examine your underlying feelings, you may find that . . .

- you're worried that your daughter-in-law won't accept and like you;

- you are territorial and have trouble letting go;

- you cannot recognize or accept that your son is an adult capable of making family decisions on his own;

- you fear you will lose your relationship or your importance with your son as the family roles shift.

Why Change?

You need to face the reality that your son's marriage means that he now has a wife. Maximize your precious family time by including her in the family. Work on improving your skills in acceptance and compromise. If you need help, seek counseling to learn how to establish appropriate and realistic expectations for your combined role as your son's mother and your daughter-in-law's mother-in-law.

Seven Simple Suggestions for Success

1. Accept your daughter-in-law for who she is and what she brings to your family.

2. Make sure to allow her to call you by a name that makes both of you comfortable.

3. Spend time together, just the two of you.

4. Tell her that you are happy that she married your son.

5. Ask for her opinion, and let her participate in decision-making when it involves family issues.

6. Learn to share when it comes to holidays. Create a plan that gives everyone a chance to host a celebration.

7. Remember that vacations are valuable, and allow time for your son and daughter-in-law to be alone as couple. Give them the space to enjoy each other.

One Final Tip

If you want to keep a close relationship with your son, then welcome your daughter-in-law into the family circle. You don't have to try to force her to love you or force yourself to love her. Just remember that your son chose her out of all the women in the world because she is special to him, and he loves her.

Learning to ignore things
is one of the great paths
to inner peace.

—Robert J. Sawyer

Keep Out
(Or at Least Call First)

Respecting Their Privacy, Home, and Boundaries

Comedian George Burns is credited with saying, "Happiness is having a large, loving, caring, close-knit family in another city." According to the women I got to know through my research, that's not always the case.

I grew up in New Jersey, and I have fond memories of our family home. One thing I remember clearly is how clean my mother kept it. So clean, in fact, that it had a museumlike feel, and my sister and I rarely brought friends home for fear that we would mess it up. This "clean house syndrome" also meant that our family rarely had houseguests. And drop-in visits . . . those never happened.

When I started dating my current husband, I realized that everyone didn't grow up the way I grew up. His door was always open to drop-ins, overnighters, and partygoers. He learned this behavior from his parents: his house was the one all the kids gathered at after school, and you could mess it up without repercussions.

It took me many years to back off the feeling of dread when my husband announced, "Let's invite so and so over for the evening"—or worse, for the weekend. My instant response was to think of the cleaning I would have to do to get ready . . . and do again when it was over. You see, I am my mother's daughter, and it just seemed like too much work. Couldn't we just meet in a restaurant or go away with them for the weekend?

> *His door was always open to drop-ins, overnighters, and partygoers.*

When we get married, some of us find a mate who isn't an exact match in the "house rules" department. Needless to say, that person's mother may not be a match either. Now that I have had two mothers-in-law with very different personalities from each other, I can appreciate the need to discuss what are acceptable and, more important, reasonable, boundaries when it comes to privacy. First, the discussion needs to take place between the new couple. If the two of them don't agree, there's little chance of smooth sailing when the mother-in-law is introduced into the equation.

So I verified that my son and daughter-in-law had had that talk; but I also knew I wanted to initiate a conversation with them before they felt the need to have it with me. According to my group of "women in the know," this seems to be the linchpin of Operation Good Mother-in-Law—or else you might hear something like . . .

Your Mother's on the Phone (Again)— You Talk to Her!

How much telephoning is too much? That depends partly on your like or dislike of using the phone. If you're like me and spend the day on the phone for business, you use caller ID a lot during your time off. I like to phone friends at times when I know I'm not going to be rushed or feel tapped out from my day at the office. I make exceptions for family because I don't want to be unavailable in an emergency. But if it's not an urgent call, I often chat only briefly and call back when I have time to relax and enjoy it.

If you're like my husband, who also spends the day talking to people but nevertheless seems to rally when the phone rings, you answer just about every phone call and seem to like doing so.

Different People; Different Reactions

With my first husband, who was one of three sons in his family, I was the one who used to regularly ask, "Have you called your mother recently?" I think "ask" really became "nag." But I didn't want to be the one who, when she got tired of waiting and eventually called us, had to make excuses for why her son wasn't calling. So when those calls came, I tended to back away from the phone.

Because I grew up in a family with only daughters, lots of lessons in family dynamics were new to me when I was blessed with sons. While it was second nature for me to call my parents to say hello, almost daily, my young adult sons call me much less frequently. And I'm absolutely fine with it . . . now. It wasn't always that way. I counted their calling home as an obligation or responsibility of our rela-

> *Communicating with them in an open, honest fashion has made everyone's life less stressful.*

tionship and felt insulted or hurt if their call frequency slipped. My sons view things completely differently. They behave just like my first husband, their father: they call when they have something to tell me, or they save up a few somethings until they have time to sit down and make the call. They phone me because they want to talk to me—not because they feel they need to check in.

In order to finally "get it," I had to stop whining about wanting them to call me more, listen to their reasons for calling me less, and be content knowing that it meant more when they did phone. No more guilt trips for my sons about calling home! Communicating with them in an open, honest fashion has made everyone's life less stressful.

I can only imagine how much this woman must hate a ringing phone after I read the following posting on the Internet:

My husband and I live in a guesthouse on her [the mother-in-law's] property to help her pay her house payment. She will call ten times a day, and seven of the times it will be all about the same thing to make sure we understand.

For example, there is a light on the porch so we can see at night. If I have that light on for over five minutes, she will have her daughter call three to four times to tell me to turn it off, even though I am still using it. Then she will call her son at work to have him call me and ask me to turn it off. Finally, after all that, I have to call her to have her stop harassing me to turn off that light, and then she complains on the phone for ten minutes and hangs up on me like a little kid.

I might consider getting an unlisted number if I were subjected to this, but there certainly are other ways to handle phone calls, as other women in my study report.

KimChi lives several hundred miles away from her mother-in-law, so phone calls are their normal way of communicating. According to KimChi:

She calls us, but not so frequently that it would annoy me. I welcome her calls and enjoy talking to her. She respects my space, and I recognize that she treats me like one of her children and not as an in-law.

When it comes to calls to and from my son and daughter-in-law, I try to remember the lessons I have learned from my research and from my experience. I don't make a habit of calling them after they've been working all day. I try to let them have that time with each other. I also am careful to respect the time-zone difference between the two coasts, especially in the morning.

Cathe, an entrepreneur who has known her mother-in-law for more than nine years, reported she and her husband's approach in one simple, clear statement: "We tell her when calling at a particular time is just way too early."

When I do call my son and daughter-in-law and get voice-mail, I leave a message that gives them "permission" to call me back whenever they feel like it. And I mean it. I don't keep a tally of who calls whom more. When they do call, I'm excited to hear from them and really do appreciate it.

When we mothers-in-law show consideration and demonstrate that we understand and respect our children's and in-laws' busy schedules and need for privacy, our conversations will be more enjoyable when they do call—and our calls will be more welcome to them as well.

Is That the Doorbell (Again)? Pretend We're Not Home!

My husband's late mother was widowed when he, an only child, was twenty-four years old. By the time I came into the picture, each of them had been on their own for more than five years. I have to admit, when I learned that she lived in our town, I was a little scared. A mere two miles from our home

> He was the pendulum that kept it all in balance. If things began to tilt, he would speak to one or both of us, and equilibrium would be restored.

seemed too close for comfort. This situation had the makings of a disaster. Would she "drop in" every day? Would I feel obligated to invite her over for dinner when I ran into her at the grocery store, knowing that otherwise she would probably be eating alone? Would she see the car outside and assume we were available? Would the following Internet posting become my life story as well?

My husband and I have been married for a little over eight years. We have three children and are usually happy. We fight most of the time over his mother. She is widowed and lives just down the street. She comes over four or five times a day, which started right after we got married. Five minutes after he got home, she would be at the door. Several years ago I found out she made her own key to our house without our knowledge from a set that was accidentally left at her house. She has no problem using it and just walking in when she feels like it. I feel that I am the outsider in "their" marriage and am about at the end of my rope. I am considering a divorce.

Any or all of those things could have happened to me . . . if my mother-in-law wasn't the woman she turned out to be and my husband wasn't the stand-up guy he has always been when it comes to me.

During the eleven years we had before my mother-in-law passed away, the three of us, plus my children, settled into a comfortable arrangement of seeing each other most days of the week, but not as a group effort. My husband would stop by his mother's house, alone, and visit with her, do home repairs, and check on her health. He saw her the most. Her visits with us as a family were planned. She never expected an invitation, and she always enjoyed just being with us, which took the pressure off of us to come up with special meals and entertainment. When my younger son, Alex, got his driver's license (the older one was out of the house by then), he would stop by and visit my mother-in-law and take her for drives. She normally drove everywhere herself, but when Alex came by, she settled into the passenger seat and went along for the ride. They often went to an early dinner as a twosome, and both of them took pleasure in their outings.

This loose arrangement worked well for us because my mother-in-law wanted her son to be happy, and my husband wanted both his mother and his wife to be happy. So he was the pendulum that kept it all in balance. If things began to tilt, he would speak to one or both of us, and equilibrium would be restored.

The story of Michelle, who has known her mother-in-law for close to fifteen years and lives near her in a small town in Italy, sounds a lot like mine. Michelle says:

I think we get on so well because we give each other space. She doesn't put any demands on me or on my family, and I don't feel any need to limit her access to or time with us. She prefers not to come to our house but always opens her house to us. She asks us to call her to be sure she is home and asks us to tell her a few days in advance if she is needed to babysit our girls. I also learned many years ago that she doesn't like calls after 9 p.m. and that check-up calls are not appreciated.

> *One thing we mothers-in-law need to remember is that we are the guests.*

If you ask Maggie, a teacher in her late twenties who lives next door to her mother-in-law, she'll tell you that it doesn't really matter where you live if the basics of understanding and respect are in place:

I can see how easily it would be for her to not respect our privacy as a family, but because she respects us she does not violate our privacy. Usually, so as not to bother us, she will call on my husband's cell phone. She will not come over without calling first and is aware of our family routines and will not disturb them. She also knows times when my husband or I will be going to her house, so if it isn't important, she will wait to ask questions until we get together.

Kiley, an administrative manager from Wisconsin, who feels her mother-in-law is a "dream come true," says:

She's very good about calling before coming. These boundaries occurred naturally because we live about thirty-five minutes away from each other and because I assume this is the way her mother-in-law treated her. Also, our schedules are busy, so if she didn't call, we might not be home.

When it comes to my son and daughter-in-law, the topic of "dropping in" is not one that's likely to need discussion, since we live three thousand miles apart. But my younger, unmarried son recently moved back to our town, and I may someday have to address it if and when daughter-in-law #2 comes on the scene. I plan to keep in mind the insights I've gained from wise-women in-laws.

She's Coming to Visit (Again)— How Long This Time?

Having my own two mothers-in-law experiences to draw upon has been really helpful in the research for this book. Mother-in-law #2 lived in my town, but mother-in-law #1 lived two hundred miles away, so when she came to visit, it wasn't a day trip. Back in those days, I had a full-time corporate job, young children, and very little free time; so those visits were scheduled several weeks in advance, and I had enough time to prepare. She was very aware of our lifestyle and was a good houseguest, never overstaying her welcome and pitching in where appropriate. We didn't have to entertain her if we didn't have the time. And she seemed to enjoy her visits. It probably worked well for me because she visited two or three times a year and never stayed longer than a week.

We made the trip in her direction with the same frequency, but usually for a long weekend, and everyone appeared satisfied with that arrangement. On occasions when I was too busy to go, my then-husband would visit without me. Sometimes he would take the kids along, and sometimes he would go alone. Nobody's feathers were ruffled when this happened, and it gave him alone time with his family, which they all appreciated.

The following posting on the Web laments the combination of a visit that lasted too long and the arrival of a newborn. How well would anyone do with this situation?

We are expecting our second child, and just like with our first daughter, my mother-in-law decided that she was coming to stay with us. The first time, we had not even been home for twenty-four hours and had my mother-in-law staying with us. I am not sure if it was just the hormones or what, but

*by hour thirty-six I was in my room crying and so depressed
that if I could have, I would have told her to leave. We live
in a small house, and there is not really any room for privacy,
but we had a futon in the spare room. Well, now that we are
expecting our second child, our spare room is a baby's room.
There is no spare room. My mother-in-law is visiting right
now and is sleeping on our couch. This bothers me a lot! My
issue is, when the next baby arrives, I want to transition from
a three- to a four-person house with my husband and daughter and without someone living on my couch. My husband
won't say anything to her at all, regardless of what I am feeling, which really makes me mad.*

Couch dwellers are privacy busters. And what's wrong with
her husband that he won't speak up when his wife needs him
to intervene? One thing we mothers-in-law need to remember
is that we are the guests.

Because my son and daughter-in-law live in Washington,
D.C., I am going to need to know how to put my visitation
skills into play.

You know that old expression "A man's home is his castle"?
Well, forget the gender reference and concentrate on the words
and what they mean. Your daughter-in-law's castle may look
nothing like your castle, and I'm not talking about the number
of rooms or the size of the property.

Each of us has our own style of decorating, our own definition of "good housekeeping," and our preferences on where the family pet is allowed to be. These topics may seem disconnected, but we'll have to focus on them if we want to avoid making our daughters-in-law crazy when we visit.

I've already admitted that I dislike clutter and have a bit of a fixation on cleaning. I haven't admitted that I have 130 pounds of dogs, housed in the bodies of two black Labrador retrievers, and they're pretty spoiled when it comes to sitting on the furniture and jumping into bed with us in the morning. For some folks, this could be a real deal breaker when it comes to visitation, and I will tell you that we have a few friends who are less than thrilled with the black hair that sticks to them like they're human magnets despite my cleaning obsession.

The point of telling this "secret" is to say that I would completely understand if my daughter-in-law—who, by the way, is a cat person—did not want to stay overnight in my home. That's why hotels should be looked at as acceptable alternatives to an uncomfortable stay in anyone's castle.

The same goes for the house layout. If, for example, having your own bathroom or a bedroom with a king-size bed in a private wing of the house is important to you, don't make your child and his or her spouse feel like they have to give up their room for your comfort. Buck up and stay nearby if you'll make yourself and everyone else miserable by staying with them.

Even with the tremendous distance that separates Twylla from her mother-in-law, Kathy, Twylla reports:

We don't have to worry about dropping in, as Kathy lives in Hawaii and we live in the middle of the Canadian prairies; but when visiting, we've always had our own room, and she'll even get us a hotel room for a night or two when we visit to give us some privacy.

After getting through house-keeping, pets, and space issues, decorating should be a piece of cake. Missy, a New York City artist, describes her experience with her mother-in-law:

Just like anyone else coming to visit, she had to come through our front door.

She knows that we are just starting out in life together and setting up our own home. She has given us design support in decorating our apartment. Louise knows we love decorative objects and antiques and is always looking out for beautiful things for us on her travels. Family heirlooms from Michael's family and new pieces that Louise finds for us add warmth to our home and help me feel connected to my husband and his family, and gives Michael and I wonderful memories to talk about.

As my advisory group has told me, even though it may feel awkward to initiate the discussion about home visits, tell the truth from the start if you would prefer to stay in a hotel. I did, because I'm allergic to cats and like a king-size bed. When preferences are brought out into the open and discussed with kindness and consideration from the beginning, your visits can be what they should be: joyful family celebrations, not royal battles for control of the castle.

She's Moving In? I'm Moving Out!

I was nervous when I first learned that my husband's mother lived in our town, but nine years after we met, I was thrilled to suggest that we build a new house with a place for her to come and live with us. She had been a great neighbor, a respectful mother-in-law, and now needed to live even closer due to her declining health. I felt no hesitation; it made perfect sense.

Before you start thinking that I was vying for the Mother Teresa award, let me say that I did not suggest she actually live in the house with us. We designed our home with a separate apartment for her, located on the ground floor. The structure had no direct access between the two living areas, but we designed it so one could be created if her health deteriorated and that became necessary. We wanted her to maintain her independence for as long as she could, and we needed to maintain our privacy. Just like anyone else coming to visit, she had to come through our front door.

As construction progressed, we had several discussions with her about how things were going to work when we all lived together but not totally together. We needed her to understand that things had to go along as they had before. She would still get frequent invitations to join us for dinner; my husband would still stop by and visit; and she would still entertain her friends whenever she wanted to and not feel obligated to include us. She understood and embraced all this and eagerly anticipated our new adventure. Unfortunately, our opportunity

> It was a bumpy road of adjustment for all three of us.

never came; she died three months before our move-in date.

But finding a way to literally live with in-laws is something many families face. These two examples on the Web are from women who seem to have big, ongoing problems in this area:

About two months ago my husband's mother moved in with us because she didn't have enough money to pay for housing and her meds. In the last month, she has become like another child that I have to pick up and clean up after. I mean, come on; she is fifty-one, and it's time she picks up after herself. She has recently started coming between my husband and me. I have heard her in the other room making underhanded comments to my husband about me. I understand that she is his mom, but I always thought that when you got married and moved out that you start a new family with your wife and kids. She has got to move out. She is causing so many problems in my marriage; it will end in divorce if she stays.

The second posting reads:

I'm recently engaged, and his parents are already trying to control my entire future. My boyfriend is twenty-five and an only child, and his parents are extremely clingy. So much, in fact, that they have already decided that after we get married, they are going to live with us. They have said that they will buy our first house for us and pay all expenses if it has an attached apartment that they can live in. This is just one huge attempt at a bribe.

I can't imagine how either of the mothers-in-law could hope to come out ahead. Although I am reading the accounts of only these two daughters-in-law, both families sound like they are on a downward spiral leading to divorce.

Faith, a licensed massage therapist, lives in her mother-in-law's home in Florida and presents a very different situation.

She is grateful that her in-laws let her and her husband live with them while they get on their feet:

When my mother-in-law wants to talk to me, she knocks on my door before coming in. If she needs help with something, she asks, not demands. And I try to do the same for her. There is no boundary on what I can and can't be included in. I'm literally like her daughter.

Several years after my mother-in-law's death, the apartment got another shot at use when my father came to live with us. A recent widower in great health, he didn't want to live alone in Florida anymore, so my husband became the saint and welcomed him into our California home. We had the same discussions with him as we had had with my late mother-in-law but discovered that it wouldn't be as easy as I think it would have been with her. He hadn't had the experience of living alone long enough to want to make his own meals, do his laundry, or look for new friends. He looked to us for all of that. It was a bumpy road of adjustment for all three of us, and after about eight weeks, he decided to be with his friends back in Florida, where he is much happier.

So I can appreciate the scenario as it plays out both ways, and I believe, as I sit here in good physical and mental health, that if alone, I would not choose to live with my children. I will take steps to provide for myself as much as possible so I don't need to rely on them for care. Perhaps the best thing about my vision of living my later years in a cute cottage with great caregivers is that it still leaves room for a standing invitation to tea with my daughter-in-law!

What I Learned: Respect Is Gained by Understanding the Privacy Ground Rules

It's never too late to discuss privacy and boundaries or to issue reminders if things aren't working out the way they were originally agreed upon. I would rather have everyone's house rules explained and understood up front, because then everyone can make conscious and considerate choices about how to adapt lifestyles to mesh with one another into one big happy family.

The Experts Weigh In

Based on my research, here are some questions you need to ask yourself to determine whether you really understand the expression "Good fences make good neighbors."
Do you . . .

- realize what time it is when you call your daughter-in-law and that your acceptable frequency of calling may differ from hers?

- walk into or visit your daughter-in-law's home whenever you feel like it?

- keep in mind that when you visit, it's their house?

- know how long of a visit is too long?

If you're having trouble with some of these concepts, you may need a little help recognizing and implementing healthy boundaries.

Why You Might Be Behaving This Way

Let's take a deeper look at some possible reasons you struggle with boundaries. You may find that . . .

- it's hard to hear "no" because you fear rejection or abandonment;

- you don't want others to hold power and make decisions that keep you from doing what you want to do;

- you feel insecure or lonely;

- you worry about your son's welfare now that he's married and living with a person who is not you;

- you feel a sense of entitlement because he's your son, and it is his home too.

Why Change?

Here are just a few of the many good reasons to work on changing your ways:

- You want to keep the relationship you previously had with your son now that he has a wife.

- You'd like to stop feeling like "three's a crowd" and discover the joy of hearing, "We're so glad to hear from/see you!"

- Mastering the course on boundaries will improve all of your relationships and help you make healthy choices for yourself.

How can you move in this more healthy direction? First, understand what is meant by "boundaries." Personal boundaries, experts say, are the limits or borders that define where you end and others begin. They help you decide what types of communication, behavior, and interaction you will accept from other people. When boundaries are healthy, everyone involved knows how to say no without feeling guilty, afraid, or angry. And everyone gets to have a sense of control and power in his or her life without feeling judged. Healthy boundaries are characterized by the following:

- being able to state opinions, thoughts, feelings, and needs with respect and to say no when you need to disagree;

- being able to be okay if others say no to you;

- having a healthy amount of self-respect and self-esteem;

- protecting physical and emotional space from intrusion; and

- taking care of your own needs.

A key learning point for me was when to set these healthy boundaries, and experts agree that the best time is before you actually need them. Once the train comes off the tracks, it's much more difficult to know how to set things right.

Seven Simple Suggestions for Success

1. If you want to see your son and daughter-in-law, call and ask when they are available.

2. If you live locally, don't just drop by.

3. Recognize their busy times and make phone calls when they can talk with fewer distractions.

4. Play by the house rules. When you visit, learn how they live and respect their lifestyle and wishes.

5. Ask before you help with dinner, housekeeping, or decorating.

6. Be flexible and understand that your son and daughter-in-law have their own lives.

7. If your son takes you aside for a talk, listen to him. It is his responsibility, for his family, to set limits with you— and it's your job to respect them.

One Final Tip

If you and your daughter-in-law have not discussed privacy and boundaries, then you have no right to complain if there's a problem. Talk openly and respectfully, and once you all know and understand the boundaries, keep the dialogue open and be amenable to change.

Relationships—of all kinds—are like sand held in your hand. Held loosely, with an open hand, the sand remains where it is. The minute you close your hand and squeeze tightly to hold on, the sand trickles through your fingers. You may hold onto some of it, but most will be spilled. A relationship is like that. Held loosely, with respect and freedom for the other person, it is likely to remain intact. But hold too tightly, too possessively, and the relationship slips away and is lost.

—Kaleel Jamison

Don't Ask, Don't Tell
(They'll Start a Family When They're Ready)

And Once They Do—They Are the Parents!

When I was pregnant with my first son, I was twenty-three years old and extremely naive. So much so that during a routine physical by my company's doctor, he revealed that the cause of my tiredness wasn't from the "iron-poor blood" that I suspected but due to being six months pregnant. Without going into details of what should have been obvious, suffice it to say that I just did not know.

Neither my mother nor my mother-in-law had yet begun to ask the "When am I going to become a grandmother?" kind of questions. And neither of them made any suggestions or offered advice on how I could successfully commute three hours a day from New Jersey to Manhattan to carry on with my career, care for my new house, care for my relatively new husband, and most important, care for a baby. I had no master plan for how this was all going to work out, and I had just about ninety days to come up with one. So I did. I would take six weeks off after the baby was born and figure it out then.

> *I had no master plan for how this was all going to work out, and I had just about ninety days to come up with one.*

Now that my son and daughter-in-law have been married for a few years, people constantly ask me when I am going to be a grandmother. My friends assume that because the newlyweds bought a house and have two cats, the next step is parenthood. Maybe it is, but I don't think it's my place to ask them. Nobody asked me those questions thirty-plus years ago; when I sprung my big news on my family and friends, it was a surprise. Now I think the way things worked out was kind of fun (even though I can't say that all of it was fun while it was happening).

A second experience also keeps me from prying into this personal part of my son and daughter-in-law's lives. When I married for the second time, I married a man who is eleven years younger than me and who did not have children of his own. For years people asked us if and when we were going to start a family, and it was difficult to deal with those questions. I was forty-five, and my chances of being able to have another child without a lot of medical intervention were slim to none.

Although we did try to have a child, we did not succeed. I'm fortunate that my husband loves my two sons as if they were his own. And I'm glad that one of the benefits of being over fifty-five is that I'm too old for anyone to ask us that question anymore!

Have You Picked a Name Yet?

When the time came to pick names for each of my sons, their father and I didn't immediately agree on any name. For our firstborn, his top picks were linked to his German roots, and to this day I still tease Erik by calling him Balthazar or Otto, names that got tossed. He did end up with a hyphenated first name, Erik-Nikolaus, and the middle name Jack, thus honoring two grandfathers.

Then the next son came along, and we decided to name him Robert Alexander but call him Alex. One more grandfather's name was adopted.

Sounds like we worked it all out pretty well, but in reality, for more than thirty years family (mostly mine), friends, school administrators, and mail carriers have rolled their eyes and questioned our rationale for giving one son three "first names" plus one hyphen, and the other son a first name that he doesn't answer to or use except on official documents.

The response to such interrogators is really quite simple: because they are our children, and we liked the names. And our sons like them too.

As I discovered from women who vented on a variety of Web sites, we aren't the only ones who've experienced "eye-rollitis." For instance, here's one battle that began before the baby was even born:

When my mother-in-law asked what baby names we were considering, we told her that we had already picked one. Even though I am not due for four months, we wanted to start calling our baby by name, for bonding reasons. My mother-in-law let my husband know right away that she hated our baby name because she once had a disagreement with a woman bearing the same last name as the name we chose for our baby's first name. She has been hounding my husband about how much she hates the name for about a month. Yesterday I received an e-mail from her saying she would prefer to have a grandson, because she can't stand the name we have chosen for our daughter. We love the name we have picked.

And another entry:

We have had an issue with my mother-in-law and our children's names. She doesn't like the names we chose, so she came up with different nicknames . . . makes me so angry. I think it is so disrespectful. Especially when it is something totally different.

Is this the battle you really want to fight with your daughter-in-law? I sure don't think that pressuring your daughter-in-law to name a child after a family member or being critical of a "creative" name, which may be a product of the era, will do anything but put a burr under her saddle.

Speaking of names . . .

Call Me Grandma . . . or Gammie, or Nana, or Mimma . . .

Settling on names can be a tricky business, whether it's for a new baby or a new grandmother, as this posting from a daughter-in-law shows:

Ever since my daughter was born, I've been fed up with my mother-in-law. Everything she does annoys me: the way she refers to my daughter as "our" bundle of joy and the way she insists we call her "Granny."

After reading that scary tidbit, I decided to have the only discussion I've had with my son and daughter-in-law that had anything to do with children: "If and when you decide to have children, what do you want them to call me? Grandma?"

It didn't seem like an unusual name request. I called my grandmother Grandma. My mother called her grandmother Grandma. My son called my mother Grandma. But he doubled over laughing when I suggested that the name seemed appropriate for me. He told me that it was a name that belonged on an "old lady." I guess I should view that as a compliment, but when I asked him for another suggestion, both my son and my daughter-in-law came up empty.

> *I know that when he is born, she will put me through a major guilt trip if I don't let her come in the delivery room.*

First dibs on names, in my mind, should go to my daughter-in-law's mother; and I recall that she had come up with a name that worked for the three of them. As for me, some of the best names I have heard for grandparents have come from a messed-up pronunciation of the person's intended grandparentlike name. So maybe "Grandma Jane" will become . . . "Grane"? Not to worry . . . I believe the answer will reveal itself when the time comes.

Grab the Camcorder . . . I'm Going In

The only people who attended the birth of each of my sons were their father and the medical staff. Back then nobody else even suggested that they wanted such an invitation. Even if anyone—including my mother and sister—had, I would have politely declined for reasons of privacy and modesty.

Times have changed. After reading several postings on the Internet, I see that it isn't that easy anymore. For example:

My baby hasn't been born yet, but my mother-in-law begged us, crying, to let her be there for his birth—which I would rather she not be. But I know that when he is born, she will put me through a major guilt trip if I don't let her come in [the delivery room].

Here's another:

My in-laws, yes both of them, were in the delivery room no more than twenty minutes after my daughter was born. I was trying to breast-feed when they walked in, and thankfully, the nurse said to get out! They came back in less than a half hour and got me on film while looking drunk from the drugs I had been given during the birth. They thought it was funny.

I can't imagine having the nerve to pull either of these

stunts, and I wonder what could possess anyone, especially the new father's own mother, to want to be so intrusive. If I were that poor woman being filmed, I'd be tempted to show up at my in-law's next colonoscopy with a video camera and then play the footage at their next family event.

If my daughter-in-law were to invite me to attend the birth of my first grandchild, I would accept with some caveats. I would not be carrying a camera into the delivery room, and I would position myself in an appropriate place to respect everyone's privacy. And if I'm not invited, I will completely understand and happily stand by in the waiting room or at home until the new family is ready for visitors.

I'm Just Here to Help

Once the initial excitement (and hospital stay) is over and the congratulatory balloons have begun to shrivel, the reality of being back in your own home—and on your own with a new baby—sets in for the new mother. Back then I had no idea what having a newborn in my life could do to rock my world. As much as I prided myself on being able to handle many things simultaneously, adding a seven-pound person to the mix who was awake more nighttime hours than daytime ones nearly drove me crazy.

My son was born in the beginning of winter, and the pediatrician strongly suggested that I wait until spring to take him outside the house. That's the way it was done in those days. So I stayed home. By the fourth week of sleep deprivation, wearing the same really funky bathrobe, and cabin fever, I begged my mother to move in with us. This scenario is funny to me now because I don't know why she never thought to ask if I needed help—she lived ten minutes away. I guess she, like my mother-in-law, thought motherhood was just one more thing I could handle successfully.

Wrong!

Postpartum depression wasn't discussed much then, but I think I might have qualified.

I did go back to work when my son was six weeks old, thanks to the help of a nanny. And when the commute got to be too much, we sold the house in New Jersey and moved to Manhattan to be able to get home to our son in fifteen minutes instead of ninety.

Through all of the child-care decisions, moving decisions, and general juggling, my mother-in-law never questioned any of the things her son and I chose for our lives. She had raised three sons while working as a full-time teacher and had done her own fair share of juggling. She understood that I had as much passion for my career as I did for motherhood, just as she had.

Although I would have welcomed any family member stepping in during those first few weeks, such is not the case for every new mother. My situation was quite different from that of the woman who wrote the following:

> *Although I would have welcomed any family member stepping in during those first few weeks, such is not the case for every new mother.*

My husband's mother drives me crazy. I am expecting our first child (the first grandchild), and I don't know how to handle her demands. I'm not a confrontational person, and it terrifies me that I am going to finally have to put my foot down on some things when the baby is born. She will be staying with us after the birth, and I'm worried that she'll step in and relieve my husband of his responsibilities.

Then I read this excerpt from Missy that made me realize how petty some things we disagree about really are—especially in comparison with this family's experience:

We have had a difficult time recently, as I just delivered still-born twins at twenty-four weeks gestation. They would have been the first grandchildren on both sides. My mother-in-law has been by our side from the day they died. She took care of me once I was released from the hospital, she made sure Michael and I both got counseling, and told us to stay strong for each other. I feel she always has our best interests at heart, not just Mike's but mine as well. She has helped put everything in perspective and helped us move forward.

Once we decided to pursue adoption in Russia, she was on board, doing research and helping in any way she can. Both sets of parents have been wonderful, and both plan to travel to Russia to pick up our children.

That helps us get perspective, doesn't it?

I have decided that the best way to handle the birth of my first grandchild is not to assume anything. My son and daughter-in-law need to decide who they want to help them, if anyone, and communicate their wishes. Whether I am asked to help or not, things will run much more smoothly if I know their expectations and can communicate with them in return.

I Never Did It That Way

It seems almost a foregone conclusion that you should know how to be a grandparent. Isn't it just an extension of all those years you spent as a parent? Apparently not, as we can see in this Web posting, which illustrates a pretty common example of the problems that arise when a grandparent gets involved in parenting:

I have a problem with my mother-in-law. She's always trying to tell me how to raise my child. She tells me that my daughter should be using the potty by now and that she should be talking a lot more. She's constantly overdressing her. Today it was sixty-two degrees out, and she wanted me to put a winter jacket on her to walk fifteen feet to the car.

I feel a problem coming on in this area. It's the same one I still have as a parent of grown men. Not the potty-training or talking part, but the clothing issues. When my sons are around, I always think they need jackets and more sensible footwear. Because I always need extra layers of clothing, even in the summer, I am convinced that *they* will be cold. I've already made a mental note to "roll with it," even if I see a pair of skimpy sandals in the winter.

The clothing thing seems manageable, but other mothers-in-law have bigger problems, as expressed in this daughter-in-law's posting:

My mother-in-law is constantly doing things we ask her not to do with our kids. For example, she buys our kids candy even though we do not allow it and never have. We throw it in the garbage and tell her that they aren't allowed, but the second we turn our backs, our kids are eating candy and drinking soda. In addition, we live in a tiny house and don't have room for more toys, so we politely asked her not to buy them except for special occasions. For the last three days, she brought the kids toys and told us that she is going to do whatever she wants.

This mother-in-law seems to be confused about whose children these are—and who gets to set the rules.

If we believe we've done a good job raising our sons, then we should be confident that they will do a good job raising their children. That means you can't blame your daughter-in-law for the rules of the house. Your son lives there too, and he needs to present a united front with his wife regarding the parameters they've set. A mother-in-law who is determined to do things her way will do just that . . . but she may be doing it minus her grandchildren, her daughter-in-law, and her son.

Lisa D. expresses her parenting philosophy—and her mother-in-law's role in their family as it relates to parenting—in a rational, well-thought-out way:

We never turn to her to resolve any differences of opinion between us, but we turn to her for emotional support for most anything we face as a couple. The primary way we include her is in our parenting decisions and choices for our two children. We confide in her regarding the ups and downs of parenting, such as when we feel we are doing a good job and when we are feeling tired or challenged. We ask her to pray or meditate on our behalf. I think the important point here is that my mother-in-law and I mutually support each other without seeking approval or making demands. To me, that is a hallmark of a healthy relationship.

Jennifer P. gave me another perspective when she said:

When my youngest daughter entered first grade very young and began to experience maturity problems, we decided to make her repeat the grade. My mother-in-law and I had long conversations about it, and she was very supportive and gave good advice . . . from her home in France.

I don't want to be a parent to young children again. I am content being a parent to the grown-up variety and letting them experience the ups and downs associated with their children. I want to be more like Elizabeth's mother-in-law:

She is a grandmother when she needs to be and an unburdened woman the rest of the time. You can always count on my mother-in-law to show up in costume and in character to my children's themed birthday parties, making her a very cool grandmother.

She also made herself available whenever possible to look after our kids so my husband and I can get some alone time.

If and when I am given directions regarding the care, feeding, and toy quotas for my grandchildren, I plan to follow them. Then maybe I'll enjoy the blessing and privilege of being asked to babysit so my son and daughter-in-law can sneak away on a date.

Who Needs a Time-Out?

One of the most difficult subjects for both parents and grandparents is discipline. First, parents have to decide what the rules are going to be in their own home, and then they have to hope that they'll be enforced when grandparents are in the picture. Consistency is the name of the game when raising children. In

> *One of the most difficult subjects for both parents and grandparents is discipline.*

order to achieve success, every child deserves to know what is expected and that the rules will remain the same with all parental role models—and that includes grandparents.

When my sons were boys, the term *time-out* hadn't found its way into my house. I'm not even sure it existed as a concept back then. I think making them sit in the corner facing the wall was about as close as it got.

I never thought that sitting in a corner in their room seemed like the way to make whatever point needed to be made. There was too much good stuff in their rooms to distract them. So I went at it a different way. I would raise my voice and my hand as I started to cross the room, at top speed, in their direction. That combination was enough to stop what needed to be stopped without going any further. And as they got older, it only took "the look" to break up bad behavior. That doesn't mean my sons instantly became angels or that they didn't get their fair share of accompanying punishments. They did. Although they are men now and their punishment days are long gone, they do occasionally still get "the look" . . . and it still works.

> *My mother-in-law had been taught "the look," and combining it with a raised voice speaking to them in German was almost worse than getting it from me in English.*

When my mother-in-law came to visit or the boys went to visit her, they knew what was supposed to constitute "good boy" behavior, but they still would test "bad boy" behavior to see how much of it they could get away with before something unpleasant resulted. What they quickly learned was that my mother-in-law had been taught "the look," and combining it with a raised voice speaking to them in German was almost worse than getting it from me in English.

As a fan of TV's *Supernanny*, I especially like the part of the show when Supernanny Jo Frost posts the house rules on the kitchen refrigerator. Even though the show didn't exist back in the days when my sons were growing up, I found that the key to successfully handling disciplinary issues was spending the time explaining the house rules to my children and to my mother-in-law. Most important, my husband was present in these discussions, and we usually had them before things ran afoul. We also recognized that as their grandmother, she should have some leeway to spoil the boys as long as my sons observed the basic rules of decency and respect.

When it comes to issues of discipline regarding grandchildren, I believe that knowing my son and daughter-in-law's house rules and, more important, supporting them, is the key to successfully navigating these potentially dangerous waters. (Allowing, of course, for a tiny bit of spoiling to occasionally sneak in!)

What I Learned: Managing Expectations Reduces Disappointments

Expectations can really wreck some great opportunities in the life of a mother-in-law and daughter-in-law, and that's especially true when grandchildren are introduced into the family. I don't expect to be invited into the delivery room, asked to move in and assume newborn care, be called Grandma, or be allowed to set my own rules in contradiction to the parents' if asked to babysit the grandchildren. I will appreciate any involvement offered to me and respect my son and daughter-in-law's parenting dos and don'ts in order to earn the right to exercise a little good, old-fashioned grandmother spoiling.

The Experts Weigh In

When researching expert advice on avoiding the "parent trap" (trying to be a parent rather than a grandparent), I found a mostly similar approach to offering unsolicited advice. Maybe that's because it's really the same tendency. Do you . . .

- think it's only fair that you be present to witness the birth of your grandchild if your daughter-in-law asks *her* mother to be there?

- hope that your daughter-in-law would like "someone to talk to in the middle of the night" while feeding the baby, and that that someone is you?

- feel that you are an empty nester, and your grandchild will assuage that feeling?

- believe your son and daughter-in-law need your parenting advice?

Ring a familiar bell? Then it's time to understand why you think this way . . . and what to do about it.

Why You Might Be Behaving This Way

Here's some insight from the experts on why you might feel and act the way you do:

- You have successfully raised your son, so you clearly know what you are doing and want to help.

- It's hard to give up control. (You've seen this one before.) You may have a sense that everything familiar is going to change again, now that your son is needed by not one but two other people. And the newest one really needs his attention.

- You're lonely and/or have too much free time, and a baby would remedy both of those problems.

Why Change?

A lot more than a tense relationship with your daughter-in-law is at stake if you don't try to resolve some of these issues. Imagine being excluded from your grandchildren's lives! Here are a few more things to keep in mind:

- Understand that a lot has changed since you had your son. Current physicians' advice, such as what position a baby should sleep in, ways to baby-proof the house, and what products to use, may be different from what you did with your newborn decades ago.

- Recognize that this event isn't about you. It's about your son, your daughter-in-law, and their new baby.

- Realize that they might need help—but that they also need time without you so they can bond, establish their own routines, and gain confidence as new parents.

Seven Simple Suggestions
for Success

1. No matter how curious and excited you are about the possibility of grandchildren, be patient and don't ask; they'll tell you when they're ready.

2. Don't expect or ask to be invited into the delivery room.

3. Offer to visit the new baby when it is convenient for the new family.

4. If visiting requires travel, plan to stay in a hotel or with a friend—even if there are extra rooms in your son and daughter-in-law's house. The new family needs their space and time to adjust to a new routine.

5. Keep your first visits short; you have a lifetime to get to know your new grandchild.

6. Ask if the new family needs help, and respond in a way that works for all of you.

7. Ask your son and daughter-in-law to let you know about their parenting practices and rules for discipline, and emulate them in your interaction with your grandchild—both when you are in their home and when your grandchildren are in your home.

One Final Tip

It is important to think back to the time when you were a new mother. For most of us, life seemed like a relentless series of questions: Am I doing this right? Is the baby breathing? Why am I exhausted? Why do these books contradict each other? Why won't he drink more? What's that new spot on her? Why do I still look pregnant? Remember feeling almost obsessive anxiety and worry about . . . everything? Be available if your daughter-in-law asks for help or advice, but give her the space she needs to work out answers to these questions and the thousands more that will come up as she and your son embark on that winding journey called parenthood.

One of the most exciting
and encouraging truths in life
is that we can always become
someone new. We never have
to settle for who we are.

—Scott Sorrell

Be a Role Model
(By Having a Life Independent of Theirs)

Inspiring by Example

When I discovered that the final secret in the journey to becoming a great mother-in-law/daughter-in-law team is for the mother-in-law to be a role model, I thought this would be the easiest chapter to write. Boy, was I wrong!

According to the dictionary, a role model is a "person to be looked to by others as an example to be imitated." I started my married life and my career in the early 1970s, when female role models in the business world were few and far between. My late mother had been a great wife for fifty-three years and a stay-at-home mom. My dad had started his own successful business and doted on his wife and his two daughters. Until I began writing this book, I considered him my only family role model.

In the earlier decades of my life, I wanted to be successful in business and be the first woman or the only woman to do such and such, stocking up on accomplishments. I was the first member of my family to attend college, the first in my group of friends to get married. I wanted to be a mom, but I was the only one in my circle who was not the stay-at-home version. I had a high-powered corporate career, believed that my work/life balance was perfect, and received a bunch of awards for my contributions in business and to women. People wrote about me and called me a role model, so I thought I knew the attributes that constituted a role model and could speak intelligently on the subject.

> *Criticizing your daughter-in-law is bad, but silence can be just as harmful.*

While doing my investigative research, however, I found this Web posting that helped me refine my focus on the subject of role models:

> *I always had role models of strong, independent, older women to guide me into adulthood; my mother-in-law, however, is a different kettle of fish.*

We don't get along, I think because she is afraid of me. I come from a different world, with different ideas. I threatened to take away her only son, someone she had depended on since he was a child. He was a boy who had taken on adult responsibility at a very young age. Her reaction is withdrawal. Her solution is not to speak to me. If she doesn't talk, the reasoning goes, she won't insult me.

Well, of course I am insulted. The apparent apathy continues toward her grandchildren. She comes and visits and then ignores them.

Stepping into the new role of daughter-in-law is difficult enough. Doing it with only a negative model to guide you in that relationship is miserable. Criticizing your daughter-in-law is bad, but silence can be just as harmful.

Reading the above entry nudged me to consult my "expert" women, and they have been inspirational in teaching me what being a good role model as a mother-in-law is all about.

Is One Role Model in the Family All You Need?

My first mother-in-law was a high-school foreign language teacher who emigrated from Germany to the United States with her husband and son in the mid-1950s. I remember their stories about Ellis Island: the three of them were among the last immigrants to officially pass through that point. She eventually had three sons, and while raising them and working full-time, she dreamed of writing a book about growing up in Europe during World War II. I heard about that book for twenty years but saw no evidence that it was ever going to be written.

Why talk about something for that long and never actually do it? That wasn't a tendency I wanted to emulate, so I did not consider her a role model. I wrote a book of my own while raising two sons and working full-time, so I felt that I had proven it could be done if you "really wanted to do it."

> *When she was a teacher, she was able to share her enthusiasm for learning with her high-school students and find happiness in her life.*

Well, in 2007 she published her book. And although she is no longer my mother-in-law, she has become one of my role models. Not because she finally got the book done but because of what the book revealed. She grew up in Germany during the 1930s and '40s, a turbulent period of history both politically and militarily. The reality of the war fought in her homeland made survival a constant struggle. At the hands of Soviet troops, she and her parents suffered periods of captivity and forced labor, deprivation, hunger, and ever-present fear. After a courageous flight to West Germany, she and her parents tasted personal freedom after many years without it. Education became her vehicle to success. When she was a teacher, she was able to share her enthusiasm for learning with her high-school students and find happiness in her life.

Elizabeth's story about her mother-in-law has some similarities to mine. She says the following:

> *My mother-in-law is seventy years old, looks about sixty, and acts about forty. She is so young at heart that she makes those of us who are still young feel old. She has had a remarkable life (especially early on, when she left her home in England during the war and traveled around the world by herself and with her best friend for twenty years). Her greatest quality is her ability to be free, independent, and unafraid.*

I never got to know my first mother-in-law well enough to understand any of the truly important details that shaped her life. Although our twenty years together as a family was a long time, I did not use the time wisely. To me, she was just a high-school teacher who was always "going to" write a book. Now I know that she really is so much more.

My second mother-in-law was more like my own mother. She stayed at home to raise my husband and got involved in school and community activities while he was growing up.

When she became a widow at age sixty, she was unequipped to run her own life. Her husband had managed the finances and, more important, made most of the family's decisions. I didn't understand how anyone could let somebody else have so much control that she would be basically helpless if something went wrong. Even my stay-at-home mother knew how to get through some of these things.

> *I would never want to imitate a woman who couldn't balance her checkbook, so she could never be a role model for me. But I was wrong . . . again.*

That's how I saw things when I heard the story. I would never want to imitate a woman who couldn't balance her checkbook, so she could never be a role model for me. But I was wrong . . . again.

I understand now that she chose to lead her married life in the way that many women of her generation did. And she remained married to her original husband, which is something I cannot claim. The fact that as a widow in her sixties she taught herself to manage her finances, figured out how to take care of herself, took charge of decision-making, and led an independent life rich with friends and family for more than fifteen years makes her a hero in my book. What do you know, another family role model!

One of my "women in the know," Shelley, sums up my second mother-in-law in just ten words: "She is one of the most selfless people I know."

And then there's my own mother, the wonderful wife to my dad and the support person for everyone in our family who seemed happy while doing it. During my first go at being a wife, I didn't think I needed support, so I didn't offer much of it to my mother-in-law or, perhaps, even to my husband in return. My second time around has been significantly different.

It was with the help of "women in the know," as well as reflections from my own experience, that I realized something important: family role models don't come in only one flavor. There are stay-at-home moms and highly motivated career women. And there are bits and pieces of all of them in each of the women in my family who have had an influence on my life.

The daughters-in-law who contributed to my research recognize that it doesn't have to be "all or nothing" when it comes to finding a role model in their mother-in-law. Here's what some of them shared:

I definitely think my mother-in-law is a role model. She put her life on hold for her children and went back to school when they were older, and she got a graduate degree and now is a college professor.
—Heather

I see the relationship between her children, and I would love to pass that type of love and closeness on to our children. Family is what I lacked growing up, and I'm so happy I have it now!
—KimChi

She makes it clear that she loves both her daughters-in-law as much as all three of her children. She respects that we might do things differently than she did or would and is also good at letting us know when we're doing something good.
—Lisa K.

She has an amazing inner calm and that can help calm me and those around me. She is a great example of a wife, mother, grandmother, and woman, overall.
—Lydie

She is an amazing role model. She is a research physician and an important person at her place of work. She has had an amazing career and worked throughout raising two boys. She was doing her residency while pregnant with both and makes everything look easy. She is such an open, fun, and loyal friend that she has so many friends and colleagues who would do anything for her. It is amazing that anywhere we go or anything we need, she knows someone to help us achieve anything we want.
—Missy

She's made mistakes and knows how to acknowledge
that, accept it, and move on. Most people I know
simply ignore their failings and brush them aside.
She will forgo time she can spend with any of her
sons individually if it could mean that they could
spend time together and works to foster family
relationships that don't directly involve her.

—Twylla

Sue is very accomplished both on the home front
and professionally. She raised two amazing kids while
working full-time. She has a graduate degree and
taught high-school business and eventually
became the first female high-school principal
in northern Colorado. Her meticulous, detailed spirit
is all for the love of family and friends, and
she believes in the power of women to say and
do and to make things happen.

—Tiffany

When I think about my mother now, I realize that she
wasn't just staying home, making meals, cleaning the house,
and raising the children. It was her ability to compromise when
necessary, listen when it was important, and be there for her
family that made her a role model. So move over, Dad, you get
to share your role as a role model with your wife.

No matter what "type" of mother-in-law you think you are,

you have an opportunity to be a role model for your daughter-in-law. Don't let a day go by without thinking about how you can set an example that both of you will be proud to embrace.

What I Learned: Let Her Dig a Little Deeper to Be Sure She Really Knows Me

A role model can make such a difference in someone's life—if that person takes the time to recognize the unique qualities each of us has to offer. By maintaining a rich and full life independent of my son and his marriage, I can show both him and my daughter-in-law that a great life lies ahead for a woman who has raised her children and launched them into the world.

By allowing my daughter-in-law to really get to know me—mistakes, retakes, and all—I give her enough information so that she can pick and choose the pieces of my life that she may want to emulate. And that same plan works in reverse. Get to really know your daughter-in-law as an individual. Nothing says your role model can't be younger than you!

The Experts Weigh In

For this chapter on role models, the researchers pointed me in the direction of human behavior, and I found that certain tendencies stood out. For example, do you . . .

- think that having a successful career is necessary—or enough—to make you a role model?

- pretend to be someone you're not, in order to impress other people?

- lack true understanding of the term *independence*?

- have difficulty maintaining your individuality and communicating it effectively?

Why You Might Be Behaving This Way

You may find that . . .

- you identify and define yourself solely as your occupation;

- you don't feel you have accomplished enough and desperately seek approval;

- you fear "opening up" to others.

Why Change?

Being a bad role model hurts the people around you—including those you love. Think about how many people in your own life have inspired and motivated you to get to where you are today. By being a good role model, you can help your daughter-in-law to achieve success in her life—which, in turn, will enrich your son's life and the lives of your grandchildren.

Seven Simple Suggestions for Success

1. Share important stories with your daughter-in-law about your life before she knew you.

2. Demonstrate confidence in yourself and in your abilities.

3. Retain your individuality: being a role model doesn't mean your daughter-in-law has to become exactly like you.

4. Get involved in something you find worthwhile: there's a good chance your daughter-in-law will see it that way too.

5. Realize that your daughter-in-law is watching you; be aware of the potential ramifications of your actions.

6. Make an effort to go the extra mile if you think you can help someone else.

7. Believe in yourself, strive to reach your own potential, and be your own best role model!

One Final Tip

Role models help us evolve into the person we want to be and help us make a difference in other people's lives. You can be an inspiration to your daughter-in-law through your example, so try to be the best person you can be. Your relationship will be enriched, and you'll all be the better for it.

A family is a unit
not only composed of children
but of men, women,
an occasional animal
and the common cold.

—Ogden Nash

Epilogue

It Doesn't Just Happen

All relationships take work. Why should the mother-in-law/ daughter-in-law relationship be any different?

It has been said that life is 10 percent what happens to you and 90 percent how you react to it. You and your daughter-in-law "happened" because your son got married to a woman he loves. There's your 10 percent. Now, how are you going to react to it?

I'm not naive enough to think that every "lemon" relationship can be turned into lemonade, even if we mothers-in-law follow every one of the steps I've learned and told you about

123

in this book. I think we can make significant improvements if we do, but a good mother-in-law/daughter-in-law relationship will take two, and sometimes three (counting your son) to keep it running smoothly.

Poet Maya Angelou said, "I've learned that people will forget what you said, people will forget what you did, but people will never forget how you made them feel."

So for my 90 percent, I'm going to give every one of these secrets a try—and I hope you will too. Our relationships with our sons and daughters-in-law are 100 percent worth it.

Afterword

Share Your Story

A mother-in-law/daughter-in-law relationship has many facets, and even after reading this book, you may have more questions. . . . I know I do. For example, what would this book look like if had I asked mothers-in-law to answer some of the same questions that I asked of their daughters-in-law? What would happen if I asked sons-in-law who enjoy great relationships with their mothers-in-law to step forward? Would they have a totally different set of "triggers" and steps that lead to success?

So many possibilities, it makes my head spin. But I have to

start somewhere, so I am asking you, my readers, to join me in the research for the next book. If you are . . .

- a daughter-in-law in a great relationship with your mother-in-law,

- a mother-in-law in a great relationship with your daughter-in-law, or

- a son-in-law in a great relationship with your mother-in-law, and

- you would like participate in my next project . . .

Please visit my Web site at www.janeangelich.com for more information on how you can be part of my "people in the know."

Thanks for your help!

Appendix

Thoughts on Birth Order and Relationships

When you conduct a research survey, you hope to find a "nugget" worth exploring in greater detail, and I seem to have found one in the results from the women who responded to mine.

While constructing the portion of the survey that would give me demographic information about respondents, I included questions about birth order. I wanted to know if the women were the oldest, youngest, or somewhere in between among their siblings, and I asked the same questions about their husbands. At the time, I wasn't sure if knowing the answers would lead me anywhere in my quest for understanding what makes a mother-in-law and daughter-in-law relationship great. But I figured the more I knew about the participants, the closer I could get to hitting on something that might be relevant.

What jumped out at me from the survey results was the

extraordinarily high percentage of oldest children married to oldest children. It blew all the other combinations out of the water. While the female participants represented a cross section of age, occupation, income, race, length of marriage, and geographical distribution, this anomaly of birth order had me both puzzled and intrigued. Could it be that the odds of having a great mother-in-law and daughter-in-law relationship was weighted in favor of firstborn women who chose to marry firstborn men? I wanted to know more, so it was time to do a little more digging.

The Birth Order Effect: Fact, Fiction, or Something In-Between

Many researchers believe that where we fall in birth order helps influence how we develop. They're also quick to add that no matter which spot we occupy in a family, other factors can influence the way we turn out.

Birth order theories also take into consideration both spacing (the time between births) and each child's sex. When there is a gap of five or more years between children or the child is the firstborn, regardless of gender, he or she is more likely to take on firstborn characteristics.

My research on firstborn children yielded lists of "typical" characteristics associated with being the oldest. Here are a few of them:

- People pleaser

- Achiever

- Perfectionist

- Reliable

- Well-organized

- Self-sacrificing

- Conservative

- Believer in authority and ritual

- Leader

- Loyal

Another common characteristic of firstborns is their confidence in being taken seriously. Many firstborns go on to positions of leadership and high achievement. Of United States presidents, 52 percent were firstborns.

So is birth order a good predictor of a good marriage? And the next logical question is, who marries whom? This is the answer that raised my eyebrows: firstborn/firstborn is a relationship that rarely happens. Firstborns tend to walk away from each other due to inability to connect.

Wow! Why are my survey respondents so different from the general population?

A Few Ideas

Let's try a few ideas on for size, keeping in mind that I am not a (a) licensed family therapist, (b) psychologist, (c) psychiatrist, or (d) research scientist with a PhD in birth order. I am a mother-in-law trying to figure out how to have a healthy relationship with my daughter-in-law by asking for tips from a lot of women who seem to have figured out how to do it.

But since this is my book, I'm going to play armchair psychologist for just a moment and put forth some potential reasons (based on characteristics supposedly associated with firstborns) why my survey came back with this interesting twist.

Since firstborn women are organized and reliable, logically, perhaps these are the women who would respond to a survey.

Because firstborn women are people pleasers, self-sacrificing, loyal, and believe in rituals, they're more likely to *try* to have a great relationship with their mothers-in-law.

Firstborn women tend to be leaders, achievers, and perfectionists, so they're more likely to address and keep working at any issues they might have with their mothers-in-law and their husbands until they achieve the desired results.

Since a firstborn husband would exhibit similar tendencies to his spouse's, he likely is confident enough to step up and deal with both his mother and his wife in an effort to please both of them.

The missing piece of this puzzle is where the mother-in-law's birth order fits in. Are the mothers-in-law in my survey firstborn too? What would happen if I had surveyed daughters-in-law who did not have great relationships with their mothers-in-law? Where would those participants fall in the birth order?

These findings deserve further exploration, with a wider survey, if we hope to arrive at more solid conclusions. But who knows, maybe I'm on to something. I can't wait to find out!

About the Author

For over twenty-five years, Jane Angelich has been a business coach, focusing on women-owned businesses; a writer; and a speaker on the topics of lifestyle and family issues. She is the author of *Picking the Perfect Nanny*. After years in the corporate world that included work for Salomon Brothers and Gap, she went on to found several companies. Her entrepreneurial success landed her more media exposure, including coverage in *Working Woman* magazine and the magazine *HomeOffice*. As one of CNBC's recognized experts on work-life balance issues, Angelich has appeared on national television and radio. She is the In-Law Relationship columnist for San Francisco Examiner.com and is the mother of two sons and one daughter in-law.